TRUMP
UNIVERSITY
BRANDING 101

TRUMP
UNIVERSITY

BRANDING 101

How to Build
the Most Valuable
Asset of Any Business

DON SEXTON

WILEY

John Wiley & Sons, Inc.

Published by John Wiley & Sons, Inc., Hoboken, New Jersey
Published simultaneously in Canada

For general information on our other products and services or for technical support, please
contact our Customer Care Department within the United States at (800) 762-2974, outside
the United States at (317) 572-3993 or fax (317) 572-4002.

Wiley also publishes its books in a variety of electronic formats. Some content that appears in
print may not be available in electronic books. For more information about Wiley products,
visit our web site at www.wiley.com.

ISBN 978-0-470-18900-9

Printed in the United States of America.

10 9 8 7 6 5 4 3 2 1

To all the members of my wonderful family,
Laura, Mitra, Daniel, Jonathan, Ian,
Matt, and Nan, who are always
in my thoughts.

CONTENTS

CONTENTS

DOWNLOADABLE FORMS

FOREWORD TO THE TRUMP
UNIVERSITY 101 SERIES

People often ask me the secret to my success, and the answer is simple: focus, hard work, and tenacity. I've had some lucky breaks, but luck will only get you so far. You also need business savvy—not necessarily a degree from Wharton, but you do need the desire and discipline to educate yourself. I created Trump University to give motivated businesspeople the skills required to achieve lasting success.

The *Trump University 101 Series* explains the most powerful and important ideas in business—the same concepts taught in the most respected MBA curriculums and used by the most successful companies in the world, including The Trump Organization. Each book is written by a top professor, author, or entrepreneur, whose goal is to help you put these ideas to use in your business right away. If you're not satisfied with the status quo in your career, read this book, pick one key idea, and implement it. I guarantee it will make you money.

DONALD J. TRUMP

ACKNOWLEDGMENTS

Many thanks to many people: Donald J. Trump for his contagious drive, unsurpassed brand-building, and ongoing support; many executives in The Trump Organization who generously gave their time to provide suggestions and illustrations and answer questions—Ivanka Trump, Donald Trump Jr., Cathy Hoffman Glosser, Meredith McIver, Jim Petrus, Suzie Mills, Chris Devine, and Jennifer Favre; Mary Moyer at Trump Entertainment Resorts; Consuelo Remert at Millward Brown Optimor; Michael Sexton, the president of Trump University, for his matchless entrepreneurial spirit and creativity; David Highbloom and Larry Morris of Trump University for our lively discussions; brand gurus Peter Farquhar and Jim Gregory from whom I always learn; at Wiley, Richard Narramore, senior editor, and Tiffany Groglio, editorial assistant, for their much appreciated sound advice and immense patience. Thanks to all.

I

FUNDAMENTALS OF BRANDING

1

TRUMP ON BRANDING
Donald J. Trump

You can't build a reputation on what you are *going* to do.
—HENRY FORD

I've been building the Trump brand for several decades and I've learned that having a quality brand is very much like having a good reputation. It's important to consider that fact, even when you are just starting out in business. Most people starting out don't even realize they have a "brand." The truth is, everything you say and do is important. Actions matter. You are, literally, your own brand whether you have a business yet or not. If you are serious about what you're doing, taking responsibility for building your own brand starts now.

HAVING A QUALITY BRAND IS VERY MUCH LIKE HAVING A GOOD REPUTATION

Being a well-known and well-respected brand name is the end result of strategy, tenacity, and a clear vision. I knew when I started out in real estate that I wanted to build the best buildings possible. Every detail mattered. It didn't take long for the name Trump to become acclaimed.

There are some great benefits to having a recognized name, especially if it connotes quality. For one thing, I can get projects going quickly now because I have a solid reputation with banks and in the construction industry. On the flip side, you can become an easy target, and people are eager to take shots at you. Everything I do attracts attention these days, so I expect it instead of being surprised by it.

We were having a discussion about the Trump brand, and all of us agreed that it has to represent the highest quality available, no matter what the enterprise might be. If I build a golf course, it has to the best. If I build a skyscraper, it has to be the best. If I have a line of suits, they'd better be terrific. I am very thorough when it comes to things relating to my brand—namely, *everything*. You need to be if you hope to get somewhere worth going.

Branding is central to marketing. People feel very confident in the Trump brand. That's why my buildings are always so successful. My Chicago building has done very well. We raised the prices way above anything they've seen in Chicago. Because of the Trump brand, my customers know the building's going to be the highest quality, the best architecture, the best management, and the best location. People buy in my buildings without ever having seen the units.

A Strong Brand Gives Customers Confidence—And Leads to Higher Prices and Higher Demand

I remember when I was building a golf course and someone mentioned how impressed they were that I would be so interested in the trees. I was surprised that they were impressed—to me it just made sense. You have to know the details yourself. Second-hand information will always be second hand. Don't be a second-hand person. Go to the source yourself. That's a start on the road to a great brand, a great reputation, or both.

TRUMP TOWER WAIKIKI

The 38-story Trump International Hotel & Tower at Waikiki Beach Walk includes 460 condo/hotel units, a two-story lobby, full-service spa, 6,500 square feet of dining and retail space, and a cascading sixth-floor waterfall. It is the first new high-rise tower and five-star project to be built on Waikiki Beach in 25 years. The Tower sold out in five hours with $729 million in sales.

"Trump Expands to Hawaii," *Multi-Housing News,* November 2006, p. 16.

Trump International Hotel & Tower, Waikiki.

Photo courtesy of the Trump Organization.

My buildings sell out before they are built. Why? People recognize the brand name and know what they will be getting—the best for their money. It's not a risk on their part. That's the great thing about building a business based on quality and integrity. It will sell itself. It doesn't happen overnight, you may have to work a while to establish your reputation and brand, but the consistency will be the standard to beat in your chosen industry. I can tell you, it's worth it.

I enjoy getting great reviews from the critics that count. For example, Herbert Muschamp, the late and great architecture critic for the *New York Times*, was not only a wonderful critic, but a scholar, and to receive praise from him was the ultimate for a builder. He wrote an article for the *New York Times* about Trump World Tower, which is at the UN Plaza in New York City. Here's what he wrote about it:

> Although Donald Trump prefers to publicize the aggressive side of his nature— it's the manly thing to do—he is also the only beauty freak at large in New York City real estate development. . . . It's not surprising that unofficial approval of Trump's building should come by way of the Museum of Modern Art. The tower embodies the Miesian aesthetic through which the Modern's design department's taste was initially formulated—I hope Trump sticks with this material. Trump does better when he ignores his critics than when he pays attention to them.

That's high praise indeed, and if your name is on the building, it matters even more. That's another great thing about branding—it automatically sets your standard very high. Who would want a mediocre product to go along with their name? No one. So right there you have set the bar at a level that requires significant and distinguished results. It's insurance against being second rate.

Another thing to consider is that the better known your brand becomes, the more often you will be targeted for criticism. Take that as a compliment, and always consider the source. Seeing criticism for what it is and taking it objectively while maintaining your momentum is a technique that is helpful no matter what business you are in.

Someone recently said that I was a product—I didn't mind the comment because the product that the name Trump represents is fantastic. In fact, if you think about it, we are all commodities to some extent. I also don't shy away from letting people know that anything Trump will be the best. That saves on advertising and I also enjoy it.

Wherever your interests lie, get started developing them now. As Henry Ford said, you can't build a reputation (or a brand) on what you are *going* to do. You have to put some action into your plans, ideas, and dreams. Trump University is a good place to start. It was set up to help you realize your goals.

Most of us need letters of recommendation now and then. I write them as well as receive them, and I always look for the words "responsible, professional, and loyal." If you can build your reputation on just three words—those words would be enough. I also think of those words when it comes to the Trump brand—responsible, professional, and loyal—to my buyers, clients, students, readers, audiences, and so forth. I'll be the first to admit it's not always easy. I am responsible for a lot of people. But high standards are high standards, and that's what I stand for. I will not accept less from myself.

In the 1980s I watched the Wollman Rink in Central Park getting renovated for 6 years with nothing getting done. I finally offered to help and had it done in a few months. I suddenly had a big reputation as a guy who gets things done—on time and under budget. People couldn't believe it could be done, but I knew better. Build your reputation around getting things done.

Start today, start now. There's a lot of competition out there, and they won't be waiting around for you. Build your reputation and your brand on intelligence, responsibility, and results. That's building the right way.

We have recently launched the Trump Hotel Collection: The Next Generation for our towers going up from Las Vegas to Dubai. It's been a terrific concept that has met with total success. My initial condominium-hotel tower, The Trump International Hotel & Tower has been voted the #1 hotel in New York City, and I can tell you that people remember the name of the hotel without much problem. Now that we've taken the concept nationally and internationally, the reception is much the same. Our tower in Waikiki sold out in five hours and that's a record. Our tower in Chicago is already 70 percent sold out with 2 years to go until completion. So if I'm enthusiastic about the merits of branding, I have a good reason for it.

There is no way we can ignore the power of branding in the world market today—so take the time to establish your brand carefully. Give it your full attention and realize that every detail and dynamic will be consequential. Once your brand name is recognizable, remember to avoid complacency. I work every single day on this and I don't let up. I think the result speaks for itself. Let your results do the same.

There Is No Way to Ignore the Power of Branding — So Take the Time to Establish Your Brand Carefully

This book is a terrific introduction to all the important ideas in Branding from a leading marketing professor who has considerable real-world experience working with numerous top companies. It will give you all the tools you need to build your own powerful brand.

Enjoy and learn!

2

WHY BRANDING IS CRITICAL TO EVERY BUSINESS

Brands are the foundation of most organizations.

Brands are your reputation—what you stand for—in the minds of your customers and in the minds of your investors. If your reputation is negative, then you will have difficulty achieving your business objectives. If your reputation is positive, then you will see the impact on your future cash flow.

Most measures in business tell you where you've been—*backward control*. Understanding brands and making smart branding decisions give you *forward control* of your business. They allow you to maximize your revenue, your profits, and your cash flow.

In some organizations, top managers understand how brands work and in some organizations they don't. It is especially important that the owner or CEO understands what brands do for their organization. If they don't understand the relationship between their brands and

9

their financial performance, their brands will likely wither and eventually their organizations fail.

In this chapter, you explore the central role that brands play in business success.

AIRLINES

PanAm and TWA at one time were well-known and successful airlines. PanAm Flight 1 circled the globe. TWA seemed to be everywhere. Neither is still in operation.

What happened? Many factors led to their demise but among them was the erosion of their brands. People knew their names—their brand awareness was high—but as their corporate lives ended, potential customers did not seem to associate much that was positive with them.

As these airlines descended into failure, they had less cash available, which meant they undercut further their customer service which, in turn, further weakened their brand, and on and on in a vicious spiral.

In stark contrast, Continental Airlines was turned around with smart and adroit brand building. Continental used to be known for consistent tardiness—often their passengers would miss connecting flights as a result. (Some said they paid their pilots bonuses for using less fuel and that contributed to the tardiness.) A new management team led by Gordon Bethune studied the market and talked to customers and decided to focus on improving their on-time performance. The first time that Continental placed in the top five of U.S. airlines for on-time performance, management presented each employee with a check for $65 and they did this in person (Gordon Bethune, "From Worst to First," *Fortune*, May 25, 1998, pp. 185–190). The former president of Continental told me that this was really like a self-liquidating premium because they saved more from the on-time performance (fewer payments to other carriers to carry their passengers on connecting flights) than the bonuses paid the employees. The result—a strong brand and a strong customer base.

THE DONALD J. TRUMP SIGNATURE COLLECTION

The Donald J. Trump Signature Collection®

The Donald J. Trump Signature Collection® includes a variety of products such as men's suits (by Marcraft), shirts (by Phillips-Van Heusen), cufflinks (by Swank), and neckwear (by Superba). Donald Trump described the suits as "better than the ones I used to get that were crazy expensive."

Launched in December 2004, at Macy's flagship store in New York City, the brand quickly became a presence in men's fashion. About one year after the launch, a Brand Keys survey of 500 adults found the Donald Trump brand among the five most-highly rated clothing brands in the United States (along with Chanel, Ralph Lauren, Isaac Mizrahi, and Victoria's Secret). The

(continued)

Trump brand was associated with "comfort, style, and fit" and with business success.

Building a strong brand in such a short time is quite remarkable. Usually, it takes five to seven years to build a brand. The Chanel brand, for example, was built over decades.

Source: Julie Naughton, "Donning Donald," *WWD,* December 16, 2004, p. 1; and Cathy Horyn, "Fashion & Style," *New York Times,* November 24, 2005.

In difficult times, it is tempting for companies to cut small expenditures from their service offerings. Recently, on a business-class trip to Shanghai, I asked a flight attendant of a major airline for a few more cashews. She said that they had run out because a decision had been made to cut back. However, what she said next was very telling—she told me, "And you know what? I don't care. I'm sick of having to try to explain this decision to passengers." She was not upset with me—she was upset with the position in which the airline had placed her. More generally, the decision to cut back on cashews (a round-trip business-class ticket to Shanghai at the time cost about $14,000) was part of the brand management—or lack of brand management—by this airline. (I think an airline should hire me—a free ticket would be nice—to keep track during one of my trips of all the little things they could do at almost no cost that would improve their brand position dramatically.)

Companies that understand their brand and its importance resist the temptations to make little cuts in costs that may have large impact on value provided their customers. For example, as their competitors cut back on meals, pillows, and cashews, Continental Airlines advertised that they were continuing to provide these small but helpful creature comforts. You look even smarter when you have competitors who do not seem to understand what they are doing to annoy their customers.

Continental outdoor advertisement.
Photo credit: Don Sexton. Photo courtesy of Don Sexton.

Main Street

The airline story plays every day on Main Street. Dry cleaners, pharmacies, building contractors, health clubs, real estate offices—all need to manage their brands for long-term success.

Our family business was founded by my grandfather. They installed and maintained water systems, including pumps, for customers such as housing developments, golf courses, and summer camps. It was a small firm—just my grandfather and my father and one assistant. Certainly they could not compete on a low-price basis with the larger firms. However, they could create a brand that stood for reliability and trust that their customers would value. My father was always on call for customers who were without water and he always fixed their problem. His customers were loyal because of his reputation—his brand.

In contrast, near the Connecticut town where I live during the summer, there was a small pharmacy—part of a national chain that specialized in filling prescriptions. They had almost no products unrelated to medications. Within two years, three national drugstore chains opened large outlets near them—one almost across the street. These stores were the typical full-line drugstores—they had pharmacies of course, but they also sold beach and lawn furniture, stationery, cosmetics, toys, personal care products, consumer electronics, food items, cameras, and developed film within an hour while you shopped. What would you predict would happen to the small pharmacy?

The competition had become more intense and so the small pharmacy could expect to lose some sales but if their brand—their reputation among their customers—was strong, they could fight effectively. Unfortunately, their brand apparently was not strong because of how they had been treating their customers. For example, once I had a problem with how they had filled a prescription and brought it to their attention. In response, the store owner made it quite clear to me that my business was not important to him. As soon as the national full-line chains came in, I switched all my business to one of them. Others switched their prescriptions as well and this small pharmacy went out of business shortly after the arrival of the chains.

Your brand represents your future earnings. Not managing your brand means you are not taking control of your future.

The Changing Competitive Environment

In the skies, on main street, everywhere, competition is becoming more intense. In such an environment, organizations must be very good at two skills—*innovation* and *brand management*.

Some years ago a consulting firm examined several industries and tracked the return on investment of firms in the industry over time. Each of the industries had key "watershed dates"—dates when a major change occurred in the industry. This type of change Peter Drucker referred to as *revolutionary* as opposed to *evolutionary*.

Industries often have watershed dates. Watershed dates may be due to any kind of revolutionary change—technological, political, economic, social, or demographic. Digital photography had enormous impact on the imaging industry. Changes in regulations have affected the financial services industry. For local businesses, changes in employment due to the opening or closing of plants or modifications of zoning laws may represent watershed dates. In real estate, changes in interest rates or in means of construction may be watershed dates.

Regardless of the reason for the change, a revolutionary change alters your way of doing business. Customers and competitors change so the skills necessary to succeed most often will need to change.

Before a watershed date is what I refer to as the "quiet time"—when customers are loyal and competitors relatively benign. After a watershed date I call the "noisy time"—when new aggressive competitors arrive and consequently provide the customers with more choices and more reasons to change their allegiances. During the quiet time, the industry average return on investment (ROI) is typically found to be relatively stable but, in the period immediately after the watershed date, the beginning of the noisy time, the industry average ROI usually declines, often substantially.

Eventually the industry average ROI may show movement upward but the initial impact of revolutionary change seems to be to depress the industry ROI. For example, over just a few years during the period studied by the consulting firm, total profits for the U.S. airline industry went from positive $2 billion to negative hundreds of millions of dollars. The decreases in industry average ROI were often due to those firms that were apparently unprepared for the noisy time such as TWA. Only when those weak or unprepared firms went out of business did the industry average ROI began to increase. Economists call this process the *adjustment process*. It is brutal because companies fail and people lose their jobs. It has occurred again and again, in industry after industry, including airlines, computers, machine tools, semiconductors, telecommunications, imaging, retailing, and financial services.

Wherever you are, in a global economy we all live in the noisy time—which will probably become even noisier.

SUCCEEDING IN THE NOISY TIME

Organizations that succeed during noisy times must have skill in two areas: (1) innovating their products and services and (2) building and maintaining their brands.

Innovating your products and services keeps you ahead of your competitors in satisfying customer needs. Leaders in imaging such as Canon or in electronics such as Apple developed new product categories that raised the expectations and satisfaction of customers. As Donald Trump states, "You absolutely have to understand what the consumer wants and how to deliver it. You've got to provide the best product with the best materials" (Jo Fleischer, "Household Name Donald Trump," *Home Furnishings Business*, March 26, 2007).

Building and maintaining your brands keeps you in your customers' minds—the only place it counts. Your brand must stand for something to the customer. Among brands of mouthwashes in the United States, Listerine usually seems to stand for "kills germs" while Scope seems to be associated with "fresh breath." After those two brands, it is difficult for most people to think of a mouthwash with a clear, well-known brand position.

Successful companies both innovate and build brands. Both skills are needed. Innovation and brand building form a dialogue. Innovation refreshes a brand while a brand allows the organization to receive credit for the innovation.

Successful companies both innovate and build brands.

Branding without innovation does not succeed. For a number of years, McDonald's had no innovative meal items and their brand was slipping. Their McGriddles breakfast sandwiches helped them reestablish their market position.

Innovation without branding does not succeed. Xerox was a major innovator in computers many years ago—but never received credit from customers and today would find it difficult to establish a brand position in computing.

The same principles of innovating and brand building apply to organizations of any size.

A printer in a small town can innovate in terms of their technology, for example, in color quality or turnaround, to remain ahead of their competitors. However, then they must make sure that their customers associate those improvements with their brand. A bank can be open longer hours for the convenience of their customers but—to receive credit—they must communicate to customers so that convenience is associated with their brand.

Innovation brings value to the customer. Branding ensures that the customer knows who is providing that value.

Why Brand?

There are many reasons for branding, such as to:

- Encourage customer trial.
- Create customer loyalty.
- Maintain prices.
- Manage demand.
- Achieve higher profit.
- Create a platform for growth.

All these are valid, but there is one very simple reason to brand:

Get credit for the value you provide.

Without credit, none of the positive financial effects of branding occur.

For example, if you go to a meeting at a hotel and they serve coffee, who gets credit—good or bad—for the coffee? The hotel. However, if they serve the coffee in cups that say "Starbucks," who gets credit for the coffee? Starbucks.

Branding consists of the attributes associated with your brand in the customers' minds. Those associations must be *managed*—as we discuss throughout the rest of this book. If you fail to manage your brand actively, then it is not clear what attributes will be associated with your brand.

Every organization has a brand—the only question is who will manage your brand. You or your competitors?

Sometimes managers complain that branding is not "fair," that customers have the wrong impression of their brand. Those managers are correct—branding is not "fair." Branding requires consistent attention and hard work to ensure that your brand has the desired associations. If your luggage is lost on a flight, whom do you blame? Most people blame the airline. In fact, it may not be the airline's fault but the fault of the company that sorts baggage at one of the airports you visited. Is it fair that the airline is blamed for the problem? No. But does the airline need to be concerned about how their baggage is handled? Yes. Because branding is about customer perceptions and, if a manager does not manage those perceptions, then they will be based on whatever information the customer receives, whether correct or incorrect. You cannot expect customers to make substantial efforts to learn the "truth" about your product or service. It is incumbent on the brand manager to communicate that truth to his or her target customers.

Branding is about customer perceptions.

Branding is not omnipotent. Branding *cannot* succeed if your product or service does not meet customer needs. There is a saying in advertising, "Great advertising makes lousy products fail even faster." Great advertising might persuade a customer to try your product, but if the product has significant shortcomings, the customer will not purchase that product again.

Branding is not omnipotent.

> ## TRUMP VALUE-ADDED
>
> ---
>
> Trump properties were compared to competing properties in several locations, including Chicago, Fort Lauderdale, Las Vegas, Panama, Toronto, and Waikiki. The Trump price premium over comparable units averaged 52 percent. The average sales velocity (units per month) was found to be nearly 700 percent higher than that for the competitors!
>
> ---
>
> "The Trump Organization Value-Added Market Study," Linneman Associates, July 2007.

The Value of Strong Brands

Try this. Write down what you think are the three or four most valuable brands in the world. Then estimate their worth in dollars.

Most managers know the most valuable brands—their guesses are usually among the top twenty brands. However, the second question—the value of those brands—they usually find more difficult. Often executives simply say "millions of dollars" or "lots."

In fact, much of what we know about the value of brands suggests the top brands are worth billions of dollars. For most companies, their brands represent their single most valuable separable asset.

Exhibit 2.1   Brand and Company Values

	(Billions of US dollars)	
	Brand Equity[a]	Market Value[b]
Coca-Cola	$65.3	$108.1
Microsoft	58.7	275.9
IBM	57.1	139.9
GE	51.6	359.0
Nokia	33.7	86.4
Toyota	32.1	217.7
Intel	31.0	114.5
McDonald's	29.4	52.6
Disney	29.2	70.2
Mercedes-Benz	23.6	68.8

[a]*Business Week,* "Best Global Brands," August 6, 2007.
[b]*Forbes.com,* "Global 2000," March 29, 2007.

Typically, once a year, *BusinessWeek* magazine in collaboration with the Interbrand consultancy publishes a list of the one hundred most valuable brands in the world. While you can debate the merits of any system that estimates brand values, there is a fair degree of consistency among the brands considered most valuable on lists developed by a variety of consultancies including Interbrand, CoreBrand, and Millward Brown.

A glance at the list in Exhibit 2.1 reveals the key characteristic of strong brands.

Strong brands are worth a lot of money.

The top brands are estimated to be worth billions of U.S. dollars. To put these amounts into perspective, Exhibit 2.1 also includes the market capitalization figures for each of the companies that owns each of the top brands. (Market capitalization consists of the value of the company in the financial markets as represented by its shares of stock.)

Sexton's Rule for Estimating Brand Value: For consumer products and services, well-managed brands typically represent 50 to 80 percent of the entire value of their companies. And for business products and services, the percentages are less but still substantial—20 to 30 percent.

Note also that some of the companies on the list, such as Disney and Toyota, own several brand names. For example, if you add up the estimated values of all the brands of Procter & Gamble, their total is within the 50 to 80 percent range.

Keep in mind that these brands are well-managed brands. The value of well-managed brands may represent a significant portion of the value of the organization. However, if the brands have not been well managed, their value will be much less in comparison to the organization's market capitalization.

Strong brands are worth so much money because they increase both unit demand and price for a product or service and that leads to higher profits and cash flow.

Brands have a similar financial impact regardless of the size of the organization. A dry-cleaner with a brand that stands for stain-removing expertise will earn more than a dry-cleaner without such a reputation. A building contractor with a brand that stands for reliability will earn more than a building contractor without such a reputation. A motel with a brand that stands for cleanliness and courtesy will earn more than a motel without such a reputation. A realtor with a brand that stands for knowledge of neighborhoods will earn more than a realtor without such a reputation. Brand building leads to future profits. That's how branding gives you forward control of your business.

How to Build a Strong Brand

In the rest of the book, you learn how to build and maintain a strong brand. You learn how to build a brand, how to rejuvenate a brand, how to extend a brand, how to protect a brand, and how to handle many other brand situations. There is one rule that is common to all these branding situations:

Keep Your Brand Consistent.

Once you have chosen a brand position, be sure that all your actions and all your communications build and reinforce that brand position consistently over time and consistently over markets. During the past 30 years, Burger King has used an enormous number of tag-lines in their advertising, nearly one every one or two years. A tag-line is not the brand, but it communicates the brand position. If your advertising is constantly changing, it is very difficult for customers to secure a clear picture of what the brand stands for. Brand communications must be consistent for maximum effect. Only recently has Burger King stabilized their brand tag-line. "Because Burger King had so many management teams, it had had so many advertising agencies, so many different strategies, I think the consumer was very confused," Burger King CEO John Chidsey explained. "So bringing back the King, bringing 'Have It Your Way' back . . . has certainly helped people talk about the brand again" ("Burger King Rebounds on Marketing," WJLA-TV, June 16, 2007).

One of the strongest brands in the world, Marlboro, initially began with the wrong target market but consistent brand communications changed that. Originally introduced as a cigarette for women, the cigarette was lipstick red in color. When that position failed, it was targeted to a very masculine brand position. The first "Marlboro men" all had tattoos. One was a SCUBA diver, another a race-car driver. One was a cowboy. The cowboy ad did so well that the entire campaign was switched to cowboys and the familiar Western Marlboro man was born—a campaign that was relentlessly consistent over many years.

So powerful were the cowboy ads that one of them did not even headline the "Marlboro" name although you can see the name on the package in the shirt pocket. In the 1990s, the Marlboro brand was second only to Coca-Cola in value and it still ranks among the top twenty brands.

Marlboro advertisements over time: Tattooed Man and Cowboys.

It is possible and sometimes necessary to change a brand position, but changing a brand position must be viewed as a major strategic decision—not taken lightly but decided only after much study and discussion. Unless there are major arguments to change a brand position, it should be consistent over time and all methods of communication should be managed to develop and reinforce the chosen brand position.

CONCLUSION

For most organizations, their brands are their most valuable resource. They represent a major asset to the organization and one that requires constant attention and management. Failure in managing brands can cause financial losses, while success in managing brands can lead to long-term revenue, profits, and cash flows. When do you start building your brands? Now. The next chapter shows you how.

3

What Is a Brand? Not Just a Name

What is a brand? Some people think it is the name or the logo. That is a very limited view of a brand. A brand is not that simple—a brand is much more than the name or the logo or the tagline.

While not simple, a brand is not all that complicated. If you want to manage your brand, you need to know what a brand is. In this chapter, you learn the key components of a brand, how they are related, and how you can manage them to build and maintain a strong brand. You are introduced to a straightforward but powerful model of a brand that you will find invaluable in making all your branding decisions.

What Is a Brand?

What is the definition of a brand? A name? A promise? A personality? A set of distinct benefits?

How would *you* define a brand? Write down your definition:

_____

_____

_____

A few years ago, I attended an Advertising Research Foundation conference on brands. Approximately 40 speakers paraded to the rostrum for their presentations. Each felt compelled to give her or his definition of a brand and, after a while, you could almost feel the audience groan from the repetition.

It was striking how similar all the definitions were. Even though each speaker used different words, there seemed to be a clear consensus among the speakers as to what was a brand.

I have replicated this situation in many of the "Building and Managing Brands" seminars which I conduct. I ask the participants for their definitions of a brand. Here are some of their responses:

- "Distinguishable logo or name that creates a preference"
- "Trust, promise"
- "Association that identifies product and is worth paying for"
- "Nature and strength of relationship consumer has with product or service"
- "How strongly consumers link your name to a personality"
- "Name that represents set of values"
- "Ownable difference that allows producer to charge a premium"
- "Name with promise"
- "A logo"
- "A name and its associations"
- "A customer's perception of a company's products and services"
- "Benefits that distinguish a product from competing products"
- "The expectations of a customer"

How does your definition fit into those listed? Most likely it is similar. Even though each manager typically gives a different definition of a brand—some emphasize the logo, some the attributes, some the clarity of the position—there is always a high degree of agreement in these definitions. When you discuss a brand with someone else, most likely they have more or less the same definition as you have!

THE TRUMP BRAND

The Trump brand has been built with great care and consistency over time. The brand's attributes stem from the luxury lifestyle of Donald Trump as well as his values of passion, drive, and enthusiasm.

The Trump name is on hotels, condominiums, rentals, casinos, golf courses, and other properties as well as on a wide variety of products including suits, shirts, neckwear, eyeglasses, vodka, leather products, business cases, residential furniture and rugs, office furniture, and education. All of these products and services in one way or another allow people to participate in the famous Trump lifestyle—at whatever level of expenditure they can afford.

As Cathy Hoffman Glosser, executive vice president of global licensing for The Trump Organization, has observed, "People aspire to own a piece of the Trump lifestyle. The products created give the Trump consumer the ability to experience the luxury of Trump firsthand at an affordable price."

Source: Paul Nanda, "Trump," *Royaltie$,* December 2006, pp. 8–9; Laura Petrecca, "For Sale: Lifestyles of the Rich, Famous," *USA Today,* January 5, 2006, p. 1; and "The Donald 'Trumps' of the Fashion World," *Royaltie$,* April 2006, p. 1.

KEY COMPONENTS OF A BRAND

There are three main components of a brand (see Exhibit 3.1).

1. *Identifiers:* The brand name, the logo, the color, the shape—anything that will lead a customer to think of the company, product, or service

Exhibit 3.1   Components of a Brand

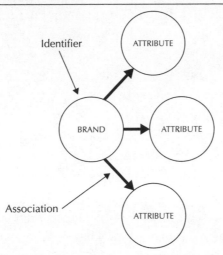

Source: "Arrow Guide—Exploring Brands," The Arrow Group, Ltd.®, New York, 2008. Used with permission.

2. *Attributes:* Whatever the customer thinks of in response to a brand identifier
3. *Associations:* The connections between the identifiers and the attributes—the wiring in the customer's mind

For example, the brand of a clothing company would consist of its name and logo associated with an attribute such as style or durability.

Brands Are Not Just Names or Logos

A brand is the name or logo *and* what it stands for in the customer's mind *and* how strong the association is in the customer's mind.

A friend of mine was in charge of changing the brand position of a well-known insurance company. That process involved changing the logo and all the content of their advertising and other marketing materials to emphasize their care for their policyholders. The final presentation of the brand repositioning plans was made before the C-level executives— the CEO (Chief Executive Officer), the CFO (Chief Financial Officer), and the CMO (Chief Marketing Officer). As my friend was talking to them, he could tell that the CFO was not on board. Finally, my friend asked the CFO, "Sir, it looks like you have a question or comment regarding these plans. Please let me know what it is so I can address it." The CFO said, "Thank you, I do have a question. In all your presentation so far you haven't talked about the company stationery. If we change our logo, we are going to have to throw away all the stationery we have and waste all that money." My friend is a quick, very savvy guy and immediately responded, "Not a problem, sir. We'll use up all the old stationery first." The CFO replied, "Well, I guess we can do this then. I'll sign off on the plan."

The C-level executives approved the plan and the brand repositioning program was put in motion. They continued to use the old stationery. But, strange things happened—employees would open a box of stationery and there would be a blemish on the top sheet so they would throw out the entire box. For the next six months, the company was using stationery at an incredible rate. It was as if the old stationery was pouring out the windows.

While the CFO seemed to equate the brand with the logo on the stationery, most everyone else in the company realized that if you change your logo and your brand position, you must make the change at once and on all marketing materials. For example, if you are sending out bills with the old logo as you are trying to introduce a new logo, you have not changed your brand. To manage a brand, you must manage all the components—identifiers, attributes, and associations. You cannot manage only a couple components but all of them at once. Branding is not just about logos and stationery, it is about the overall *perceptions* in the minds of your customers.

A brand is not just a name or logo.

As you manage your brand, keep in mind the brand model in Exhibit 3.1. That model is used throughout this book as a framework for making many types of branding decisions such as building brands, rejuvenating brands, extending brands, and handling brand crises. The model is based on both common sense and research. Because it is straightforward, you will also find that it is very helpful when explaining to others just what a brand is.

Identifiers

Identifiers include name and logo but may be anything that brings your brand to mind to your customers. Color may be an identifier such as Kodak yellow, IBM blue, or Avis red. Shape may be an identifier—the shape of the classic Coca-Cola bottle and the BMW grill. Taste—for many years Listerine mouth wash was known for its unpleasant taste. Aroma—KFC and Mrs. Field's both employ aromas to alert customers to the presence of their brands. Timex has employed for many years the tagline, "It takes a licking but keeps on ticking," while Wal-Mart uses "Save Money. Live Better." and Target uses "Expect More. Pay Less." Any distinctive characteristic can serve as the identifier for a brand.

Some people—including some brand consultants—still consider a brand as consisting only of the name and logo and therefore they tend to think of brand-building as graphic design. While graphic design is important to brand-building efforts, it is just part of the process that also involves choosing the brand's attributes and building associations by communicating the desired attributes consistently over time.

Originally brand identifiers emerged so that customers could identify the producer of a product. For example, identifiers flourished especially during the Industrial Revolution because products were sold a considerable distance from where they were produced. In the 1980s, branding and advertising were developing rapidly in China. Bicycles—a major mode of transportation then—had wonderful brand names such as "Flying Pigeon" and "Plum." Where did these names come from? Often they came from the attributes of the bicycles. For example, a Flying Pigeon bicycle was very fast and a Plum bicycle was very beautiful. What was an "Everlasting White Mountain" bicycle like?

Strong and sturdy for carrying heavy loads. Even if a company does not manage a brand name, customers will form a perception of what the product or service stands for and that will become the brand position.

How important is consistency of the identifiers? Very important. The Mandarin Hotel chain includes some of the most highly rated hotels in the world. A number of years ago, each hotel in the system was using its own logo and its own advertising. Without consistency across locations, there was no way to build a common brand position for Mandarin Hotel and of course there were no economies of scale in their branding activities because all the messages from all the hotels differed. Their advertising agency led an effort to unify their brand-building by

Be part of the legend in Hong Kong.

MANDARIN ORIENTAL
HONG KONG

After your first stay at Mandarin Oriental Hong Kong you probably couldn't imagine anything that would impress you more. But something will. Your second visit. Because we'll remember your name. Your favourite drink. Even how many pillows you prefer. It's this unobtrusive attention to individual service that makes us one of the finest hotels in the world and has earned us the reputation of the legend. We know you wouldn't want it any other way.

MANDARIN ORIENTAL
THE WORLD'S FINEST HOTELS

Mandarin Oriental (Hong Kong) Hotel advertisement.

developing a logo for the chain—an oriental fan that would be used by all the hotels. Just by changing and unifying the logo—with no increase in advertising spending—in one year the chain's occupancy rate increased approximately 40 percent! Individual hotels were allowed to advertise their catering services locally but in all communications to business travelers in media such as airline magazines, the oriental fan was employed.

Attributes

Attributes can be many things (see Exhibit 3.2). They are whatever comes to the customer's mind when they are exposed to one of the brand's identifiers. Usually, the first attribute people associate with a brand is the product or service. However, you hope that they will associate the product or service with a benefit or need because that will have an impact on whether people purchase or not. The attribute may be positive (hopefully), but it can be negative.

What comes to mind when you see the following brand names: Toyota, Pepsi, Crayola, BP, Nokia, Avis, Haier, Samsung, Citi, Ikea, Heineken, Chanel, Sony, Lufthansa, Budweiser, Michelin, DuPont, Dell?

Exhibit 3.2   Types of Attributes

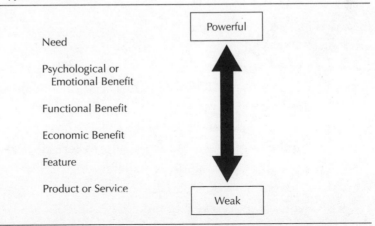

Source: "Arrow Guide—Brand Challenge," The Arrow Group, Ltd.®, New York, 2008. Used with permission.

Most likely your first thought is of the product or service associated with each brand. Cars for Toyota, soft drinks for Pepsi, and crayons for Crayola. That your customers know what your company does is helpful but it does not provide the differentiation needed for a brand to be powerful.

Sometimes a brand causes customers to think of features. Zip-Loc bags, for example, may lead customers to think of a kind of bag closing and an Intel chip may bring to mind processor speed. While you hope that your customer knows the features of your product or service, that information may not lead them to try or buy your product or service.

To persuade customers to purchase and use your products or services, the brand attributes should be a benefit you provide or a need you satisfy and must be based on the positioning of your product or service. Benefits are dimensions of your customer's problem such as a comfortable ride on a bus; features are specifications such as the bus suspension.

Brand positions should consist of benefits or needs—customers buy benefits not features.

Associations

Associations are the relationship between the identifiers and the attributes. Powerful brands have strong associations. It is not just the existence of attributes that affect customer behavior—the links between the identifiers and the attributes need to be strong in the customer's mind. For example, the attributes of Wal-Mart—"everyday low prices"—and Target—"affordable style"—may be more tightly connected to their brand names and therefore more clearly understood than the attributes of competing retailers such as Sears and Kmart. That may account for their relative success.

When you see or hear of a brand, how long does it take for you to think of an attribute associated with the brand? The less time it takes, the more strongly the brand is associated with that attribute. For example, if you see McDonald's or Burger King or Wendy's, you will almost certainly think of hamburgers. If you see Harry's, you may not think of hamburgers—unless you happen to be from Connecticut, as I am, where Harry's is a legendary hamburger stand in the southeast part of the state.

With strong brands, there is little mental pause between the identifiers and the attributes. Strong associations between identifiers and attributes mean you are getting credit for those attributes in the customer's mind. Attributes affect the behavior of your target customers *only* if they are strongly associated with the identifiers.

When you thought of any of the brands mentioned earlier— Toyota, Pepsi, Crayola, BP, Nokia, Avis, Haier, Samsung, Citi, Ikea, Heineken, Chanel, Sony, Lufthansa, Budweiser, Michelin, DuPont, Dell—how quickly did the attributes come to your mind?

Think of some local businesses. How quickly do their attributes come to mind?

You can test the strength of brand associations with reverse associations. For example, if I say "courtesy," what airlines come to mind? If I say "user-friendly," what software comes to mind? If I say "sound financial counseling," what brokers come to mind? If I say "Scotch whiskey," what brand comes to mind? Chivas Regal once tried using associations in reverse in their brand communications—in one ad asking "What Scotch will be served?"

Or try the same questions on a local basis. If I say "reliable," what electrician comes to mind? If I say "wide selection," what retailers come to mind? If I say "accessible," what physicians come to mind? Think of businesses you know—your dry-cleaner, your accountant, your dentist, your favorite pizza restaurant. What attributes do you associate with each of them? Do they have clear personalities? Is it clear what they stand for?

Building Associations How do you build strong associations? With consistency, over time, and over markets.

Suppose I say "Kodak." What do you think of? Most likely film. Notice, though, that Kodak has spent huge amounts of advertising

Guess what Scotch is about to be served.

Chivas Regal advertisement: "Guess which Scotch is about to be served."

money worldwide and over many years trying to get people to say "Memories" when they hear Kodak. Building associations can be expensive and time-consuming.

In the United States, the brand of Foster's beer has been built as "Australian for Beer." This association has been accomplished with many, humorous and very short—15-second—spots explaining "How to Speak Australian" bolstered by outdoor ads. By focusing on "Australia," Foster's has created a very efficient way to build their brand. Australia has many positive qualities, such as friendliness and honesty, which create a unique brand position for Foster's beer.

Incidentally, in Australia, the best-selling beer is not Foster's—it's Victoria Bitter or VB. You could argue that there is a more logical and persuasive argument for VB to be "Australian for Beer" than for Foster's. However, if VB were introduced in the United States, it would be difficult to use the "Australian for Beer" position for VB—even though they have a stronger argument for that position than does Foster's. Once Foster's has taken that association, it would be very difficult for another brand to own that. Associations should be built as soon as possible so that a competitor cannot claim them.

Generally, do not expect to build strong associations between your identifiers and more than two or three attributes. Branding requires you to make choices as to which attributes to concentrate on. While marketing typically allows discussion of all the benefits of a product or service, branding requires concentration on just those benefits that you believe will have the most impact on your target customer.

Do not try to associate more than two or three attributes with your brand.

I was at a branding convention in Chicago and a woman approached me during a break. She said, "I'm with a telecom company and our CEO has declared that our brand must be seen as trustworthy, loyal, helpful, friendly, courteous . . . cheerful, thrifty, nearly the whole Boy Scout oath. Is that possible?" Probably not. It would be very unlikely to connect all those attributes to the brand—it's just too much for a customer to learn. When I advised GE on their branding, I suggested that they were trying to connect far too many attributes to the GE brand.

Branding requires you choose a few key attributes for your position. If the brand position involves too many attributes, it will be unclear to the target customers. If you try to tell everyone everything, you will end up not telling anyone anything.

Think of the attributes you would like your target customers to associate with your brand. When they hear or see your brand name, what attributes do they think of? Are those the attributes you want them to associate with your brand?

Left-Hand Side and Right-Hand Side Associations Associations not only include those connected to the brand, they also include associations between your customer's problem and the product or service (see Exhibit 3.3).

The right-hand side problem for a brand manager consists of building the associations with those brand attributes that comprise the brand's position. What I call the manager's left-hand side brand problem is linking your product or service or, better, your brand to your customer's problem so that they will consider your brand when they are about to purchase. Some brands that have succeeded in developing strong right-hand side associations fail because the left-hand side associations have not been developed.

Exhibit 3.3 Associations

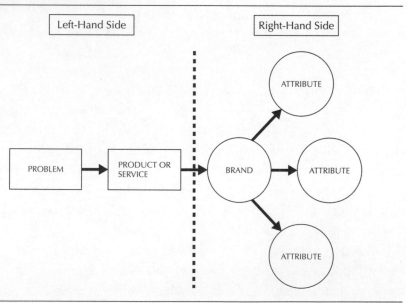

Source: "Arrow Guide—Exploring Brands, " The Arrow Group, Ltd.®, New York, 2008. Used with permission.

The association between problem and product or service determines whether the customer will even consider your product or service category as a possible solution to their problem. For example, if someone needing urban transportation does not even consider subway transportation, then, regardless of the brand attributes of subways, they will have no impact on that customer. Or if someone needing exercise does not consider a health club, the benefits of a specific health club will have no impact. Examples of left-hand side brand advertising include various foods such as beef ("It's What's for Dinner") and milk ("Got milk?")—brand campaigns designed to persuade customers to think of those product categories. In Australia, Kellogg's used a left-hand side campaign to develop the breakfast cereal market and, in the United Kingdom, the Royal Mail increased demand for their services by showing situations and occasions where e-mail would just not work—their "What would you send?" campaign.

Left-hand side advertisements: Royal Mail (United Kingdom) and Kellogg's (Australia).

The association between product or service and your brand determines whether or not your brand is in the customer's considered set—the set of brands from which they will make their final choice. If you are shopping for a car and do not even think of a particular make of car, then, no matter how effective their right-hand side brand communications are, you will never see them and they will have no effect. Ford was very successful with the left-hand side slogan, "Have you driven a Ford lately?" designed to invite car buyers to return to Ford showrooms.

Miller Brewing introduced the first successful low-calorie beer in the United States and quickly dominated the bar market. When someone asked for a light beer in a bar, they would almost always get a Miller Lite. Budweiser changed that by working on the left-hand side associations. They ran a series of television advertisements where someone in a bar asked for a "light" and a train lantern or Aladdin's lamp came sliding down the bar. The patron then quickly said, "I meant a Bud Light" and received a Bud Light instead. The ads rewired the associations in the customer's head so that "light" no longer automatically meant Miller Lite.

When building a brand, you need to look at all the associations that lead to a purchase of your product or service—both left-hand side and right-hand side associations.

CONCLUSION

Brands consist of identifiers, attributes, and associations. They must be managed together. Changes in any component of a brand change the brand. The basic principle of managing a brand is to be consistent. Consistent in communications. Consistent in behavior. Consistent in all the ways you do business. Inconsistencies break the brand promise and confuse the customers. Consistent actions build a powerful and valuable brand.

4

YOUR BRAND POSITIONING

Positioning is the heart of your brand strategy. If your positioning is unclear or off the mark, your brand strategy will not succeed. Effective positioning requires an understanding of your customer's needs and an understanding of what you do well. If there's a match, your brand should succeed.

In this chapter, you learn the fundamentals of developing a strong position for your brand.

TRUMP™ SUPER PREMIUM VODKA

Entrepreneurship requires great products. Trump™ Super Premium Vodka received a "4-Star Highly Recommended" rating from F. Paul Pacult's *Spirit Journal,* which does not accept advertising nor charge fees for reviewing products in published reviews. The journal's publication costs are paid for by subscriptions. The review

(continued)

Trump™ Super Premium Vodka
Photo courtesy of the Trump Organization.

said in part, "Clear appearance; superb clarity. The first nosings after pour reveal dry, earthy scents of grain and paraffin. . . . Finishes elegantly, oily/cream, and snack cracker-like. You're NOT fired. . . . HIGHLY Recommended."

Trump™ Super Premium Vodka was also recently awarded a "Superb (90 to 95) Highly Recommended" rating from *Wine Enthusiast Magazine.*

Trump™ Super Premium Vodka is produced by Drinks Americas, in partnership with The Trump Organization. Its launch in late 2006 was one of the most successful spirit launches ever, with over 100,000 cases sold in the first 12 months of sales.

Drinks Americas signed an agreement with Recolte to be their exclusive distributor in Russia where the vodka market is expected to be worth over U.S. $20 billion by 2009. Patrick Kenny, president and CEO of Drinks Americas, noted that, "The Russian consumer is aware of Donald Trump's accomplishments and his reputation for excellence. They respect his entrepreneurial accomplishments and they appreciate great vodka."

Source: "Trump Super Premium Vodka Receives 4 Star Rating from F. Paul Pacult's *Spirit Journal*," Sys-Con Media, July 7, 2007; and "Drinks Americas Expands Trump Super Premium Vodka to Russia," Drinks Americas Holdings press release, November 5, 2007.

THE BRAND POSITION

Brand positions consist of a few benefits that your customers want and you can provide. Brand positions can be built on *economic benefits* such as low prices as, for example, Wal-Mart does in retailing and GEICO in auto insurance. Economic benefits can be a powerful position for budget-conscious target customers. *Functional benefits* refer to how well a product or service performs and also can be the basis for strong brand. The initial and very successful brand position of FedEx was "Absolutely, positively overnight." American Tourister focused on the strength of their luggage.

Emotional benefits often are the most powerful benefits on which to build a brand because they are usually more difficult for competitors to imitate than functional benefits. For example, if a fast-food chain touts their cooking method—that can be copied. If they focus on their ambience—a place to relax—that position is more difficult to copy. Emotional benefits also may have more impact on behavior—functional benefits appeal to the mind, emotional benefits appeal to the heart and often the heart rules the mind. For many years, Michelin has linked their tire brand to the safety of your children.

Some of the strongest brand positions are built on needs such as health, status, and lifestyle. Brands such as Louis Vuitton and Harley-Davidson are powerful because they relate to deep concerns of customers. In advertisements around the world, Johnson's products are linked to the welfare of babies.

American Tourister and Michelin advertisements.

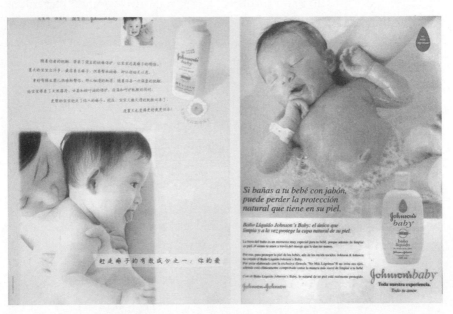

Johnson's Baby Product advertisements (China and Latin America).

Evaluate your brand position. The brand attributes in your positioning should be:

- Important to your target customer
- Benefits you provide at a level superior to that of your target competitor

Picturing Your Brand Position

You can picture the position of your brand relative to those of your competitors with a *perceptual map*. For example, in Exhibit 4.1, the two axes correspond to the two most important benefits of your product or service for your customers in a specific target market. (You would create other perceptual maps if you were interested in more than two benefits.)

You can develop a perceptual map by asking your customers to evaluate your brand and competing brands according to how they perform on each of those two benefits. You can begin by using your own knowledge of your brand and your competitor's brand to develop the chart. However, at some point you need to ask your customers for their opinions.

Exhibit 4.1 Perceptual Map: Auto Repair Shops

```
                    Benefit 2: │ Excellent        Ideal
                    Promptness │                  Point

                         A     │
                         B     │
                               │
            Poor               │                  Excellent
         ──────────────────────┼──────────────────────────
                               │                  Benefit 1:
                               │                  Courtesy
                               │
                               │            C
                               │
                               │ Poor
```

In addition to asking your customers to compare existing brands, you can also ask your customers what they consider to be the ideal product or service—that is known as the *ideal point* for those customers.

From a perceptual map, you can see which brands are your closest competitors. A perceptual map also shows you where there may be gaps in the marketplace.

Suppose that the perceptual map in Exhibit 4.1 described customers' opinions regarding the automobile repair shops in an area and that the two highest priority benefits were courtesy (benefit 1—higher courtesy on the right) and promptness in making the repairs (benefit 2—shorter times at the top).

As you can see, shops A and B are relatively fast but not very courteous. Shop C is relatively slow but more courteous. ("We are very sorry it is taking much longer than we thought to fix your cooling system.") According to the perceptual map, there are no existing brands near the ideal point—courtesy and prompt service. That gap would likely indicate a market opportunity for a new auto repair shop.

Dominant Brands

Brands that are dominant have a brand position that *owns* an attribute. Kleenex, Jello, Xerox, Kodak, Band-Aid, and Q-tips are dominant brands. Many people think of safety when they hear Volvo. Hershey makes people think of chocolate and Harley-Davidson may bring to mind freedom. These attributes provide information and affect what customers purchase.

It can be valuable to have a dominant brand. You would like to own an attribute if customers value that attribute. However, there are disadvantages to dominant brands—they may be difficult to rejuvenate (Chapter 11) or extend to other product or service categories (Chapter 12).

A brand can also be *too* dominant—so dominant that the brand name is lost. Linoleum and kerosene were once brand names but became synonymous with the product and so became generic names. Kleenex, Jell-O, FedEx, and Band-Aid all face this problem. And one

Volvo outdoor advertisement (Hungary).
Photo credit: Don Sexton. Photo courtesy of Don Sexton.

never "xeroxes" letters at the Xerox Corporation—you *photocopy* letters because using your brand name as other than a proper name may start the process of the brand name becoming a generic name. If a court were to decide your brand name was generic, then you would have lost a huge amount of corporate value.

Multiple Brand Positions

Brands should not try to occupy two distinct positions at the same time. Multiple brand positions confuse the customer. In Chapter 17, when we discuss building a personal brand, one of the principles given for developing an effective resume is to tailor it to the position in which you are interested and be careful not to prepare a resume that says everything you are capable of doing. Such a broad-ranging resume would quite possibly confuse the recruiter as to your key skills.

> **A brand with multiple positions may confuse the customer.**

PS/ValuePoint advertisement (Hong Kong).
Photo credit: Don Sexton. Photo courtesy of Don Sexton.

Multiple positions can harm your master brand. At one point, IBM sold several different brands of personal computers. One was called Value-Point. It was a personal computer cheaper than the IBM model personal computers. However the ads, such as one on a Hong Kong billboard, stated that it was an "IBM ValuePoint," confusing the IBM brand with the ValuePoint brand. That helped the sales of ValuePoint personal computers but likely had a negative affect on the sales of IBM computers.

WHO IS THE CUSTOMER?

Your brand positioning should be directed to persons not to groups. Often the customer decision involves more than one person and you should consider tailoring your brand position to specific individuals in that decision-making process.

The customer is anyone involved in the purchase decision.

All the people involved in a purchase decision in any way comprise the *decision-making unit*. Different individuals may play different roles in the decision-making unit:

- *Initiator*—Begins the process. "Our old computer is just so slow."
- *Gatekeeper*—Manages the information that the decision-making unit sees. "I saw an ad for a computer that I think would be great for us."
- *Influencer*—Has an interest in the outcome of the decision. "Any computer we buy needs to be faster."
- *Decider*—Makes the final decision but with the advice of the other members of the decision-making unit. "I think this computer is the best deal for us."
- *Vetoer*—Can stop the purchase. "My friend had one of those computers and said you never could talk to their customer support people."
- *User*—Uses the product. "I am going to do the household finances on the new computer."

A decision-making unit member may play more than one role. The person who starts the process to purchase a new computer may be the one who uses it the most.

When you position your brand, you need to think about on whom in the decision-making unit you will concentrate your efforts. Each member of the decision-making unit may want different benefits—one may want more speed, another may want superior graphics. Usually you cannot be everything to everyone, so you need to select someone to whom your brand will have strong appeal and you do that by associating your brand with the attributes they want.

PERCEIVED VALUE

Perceived value summarizes the power of your brand. Perceived value is the maximum the customer is willing to pay for your product or service and depends on how attractive your brand positioning is to

Exhibit 4.2   Perceived Value

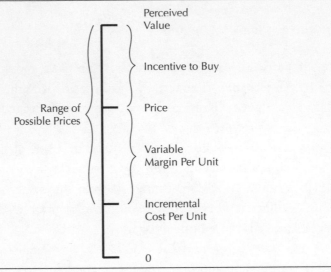

Source: "Arrow Guide—Pricing Analysis," The Arrow Group, Ltd.®, New York, 2008. Used with permission.

your customer *and* how well you have communicated that position to your customer.

Perceived value is *not* your price but is the *ceiling* on your price. If you were to try to price above perceived value, your customer would not buy. Pricing just below perceived value leads to a high margin but provides little incentive for your customer to buy (Exhibit 4.2). The lower your price, the more incentive you provide the customer to purchase your product or service.

Perceived value is central to marketing. Every activity in marketing—positioning, segmentation, branding, advertising, selling, distribution, pricing—is focused on perceived value.

> **Perceived value is the maximum your customer will pay.**
> **All of marketing is the management of perceived value.**

Perceived value depends on three things:

1.   The benefits you provide

2. The performance on those benefits by you and by your competitors *as perceived by the customer*
3. The relative importance of each of those benefits to the customer

Benefits include what your customer experiences as they use your product or service. They also include what benefits they believe you provide—the attributes associated with your brand. The perceived value of any product or service is due to the benefits experienced and the benefits associated with your brand. For luxury products or services such as fragrances and top-tier restaurants, the brand-related benefits likely represent 80 percent to 90 percent of the perceived value of your product or service! For utilitarian products or services such as cement and low-tier hotels, the brand-related benefits likely represent a much lower percentage of perceived value, perhaps 10 percent to 20 percent (see Exhibit 4.3).

You can estimate perceived value in monetary terms with various statistical techniques. In practice, you can get an approximate idea of the perceived value for your brand by looking at the prices of competing products or services with similar characteristics.

The stronger your brand, the higher your perceived value and the higher your sales and profits. Selecting attributes of importance to

Exhibit 4.3   Brands and Perceived Value

Product Category	Percentage Perceived Value
Perfumes	98
Cookies	90
Oil	85
Cars	75
Audit	60
Telephony	49
Hotels	40
Draft beer	30
Gasoline	14
Semiconductors	5

Source: Interbrand presentation at Columbia University, 2000.

your customers and associating them with your brand identifiers builds a strong brand and helps you achieve your financial objectives.

STRATEGIC THEMES

The strategic theme matrix (see Exhibit 4.4) shows the two major dimensions of any company's strategy: value and cost. Cost is the delivered cost per unit to the customer. Note that it is cost to the company—not price to the customer. A lower cost enables a company to charge a lower price but just because they have low costs, they may not set low prices. Value refers to perceived value—the maximum the customer is willing to pay for your product or service and which, like costs, can be expressed in monetary terms.

The most powerful and profitable position on the strategic theme matrix is clearly the upper right-hand corner—highest perceived value and lowest per unit cost. However, research has shown that companies also win in the middle position in the top row—highest perceived value with acceptable per unit cost—or in the middle position of the

Exhibit 4.4   Strategic Themes

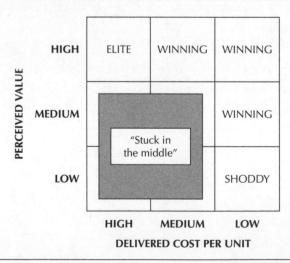

Source: "Arrow Guide—Exploring Brands," The Arrow Group, Ltd.®, New York, 2008. Used with permission.

right-most column—acceptable perceived value at lowest per unit cost. Where one does not want to be are the four cells in the lower left—what Michael Porter of the Harvard Business School has described as "stuck in the middle"—positions without either highest perceived value or lowest per unit cost. Companies stuck in the middle lose share to both the high value and low cost companies.

You can make money with elite products (highest perceived value and highest per unit cost) but these tend to be high-margin, low-volume businesses. You can also make money with shoddy products or services (lowest perceived value and lowest per unit cost) but you probably would not want to risk your well-known brand name on such a business.

Branding decisions affect your perceived value and allow your organization to move in the vertical direction on the strategic theme matrix. That is what Continental Airlines did. Continental Airlines conducted surveys to learn what customers wanted from an airline. They fixed their service and then communicated their changes to their customers.

Southwest and Jet Blue also understand customers and have put considerable competitive pressure on many airlines who find it difficult to be customer-focused (regardless of their advertising promises). Southwest Airlines is one of the few organizations that has achieved the position at the upper-right corner of the strategic theme matrix—the most powerful position. Their financial performance reflects both their brand capabilities and their operations capabilities.

The remaining chapters in this book discuss how to strengthen your brand and increase your perceived value.

Conclusion

Brands affect customers because of the attributes associated with them. The more important is the attribute—benefit or need—and the higher the level at which you provide it, the more impact you will have on your customers.

Customers will choose your brand if they believe that your product or service can satisfy their needs and if they associate your key attributes with your brand. The brand position is the heart of your brand strategy. Strong brand positions lead to strong perceived value that leads to strong financial performance.

5

How Service Branding Is Different

Services are different from products.

Overall you develop the brand strategy for a service and for a product with a similar approach. For both, you need to determine the target markets and select the attributes that comprise the positioning for your brand. Where branding services and products differ typically is in the programs used to implement the branding strategies. When you are branding a service such as a realty office or a store, you need to be aware of these differences and how they might affect your overall branding plan.

In this chapter, you consider all the ways branding services require your special attention.

At each property of the Trump Hotel Collection, there is an Attaché Department, headed by an Attaché Guest Services Manager. Their responsibility, according to Jim Petrus, chief operating officer of Trump International Hotel Management LLC, is "to personalize the guest experience . . . [and] create the sense that every guest and owner is a VIP, and each stay a return 'home,' where desires are intuited and requests anticipated."

Members of the department are prepared to handle virtually any guest request such as:

- Arranging for a personal trainer
- Shopping for gifts and souvenirs
- Providing secretarial services
- Accommodating pets
- Stocking kitchens with favorite groceries
- Recruiting a chef to provide a private dining experience
- Securing private access to salon services

Guest preferences are carefully recorded in a detailed guest history that is referenced and updated on each visit.

The service goes beyond the usual concierge service. First introduced in 1997 at the Trump International Hotel & Tower New York, the program has been refined to ensure high-level service for every guest and resident.

"Trump Attaché," The Trump Organization press release, October 10, 2007.

WHAT IS A SERVICE?

The simplest definition of a service:

A service is any action of value one can perform for another person or organization that does not result in ownership.

Just as there is an enormous diversity of products, there is an enormous diversity of services. Rarely is there a "pure" service or a "pure" product. Nearly all products involve some kind of service. Nearly all services involve some kind of product.

Services often need products to enable the services. For example, airlines require airplanes and contractors require earth-moving equipment. Education requires products in the form of some way for student and teacher to communicate—whether it's on the famous log where Socrates' students sat or an Internet connection with Trump University.

Products often involve service before, during, or after the transaction. Suppose, for example, you run a small men's clothing store. Before the sale of a suit, the customer may be looking for advice regarding style and materials. During the sale, the customer solicits opinions regarding how the suit looks on him. After the sale, there may be a need for alterations. How each of these services is handled affects not only the enjoyment of the suit purchased but often whether the customer returns to make another purchase.

DIFFERENCES BETWEEN SERVICES AND PRODUCTS

The main differences between products and services concern:

- Degree of contact with the customer
- Intangibility of benefits
- Perishability of benefits
- Involvement of the customer in operations

Each of these differences affects how you will implement your service branding strategy.

Degree of Contact with the Customer

The heart of the service business system is the *service encounter.* That is the interaction between your customer and your organization's contact people (see Exhibit 5.1).

You may provide the service directly to your customer as with a real estate transaction or brain surgery. Or you may manage the relationship for a service that will be performed later such as dry-cleaning or an airline flight.

> **To the service customer, your contact people are your brand.**

In contrast, in the product business system, products are produced at a manufacturing facility usually without the customer being present

Exhibit 5.1   The Service Business System

PURCHASE
DECISION

PRODUCTION

USE

CONTACT
PEOPLE

QUEUE

CLIENT

The Service Encounter

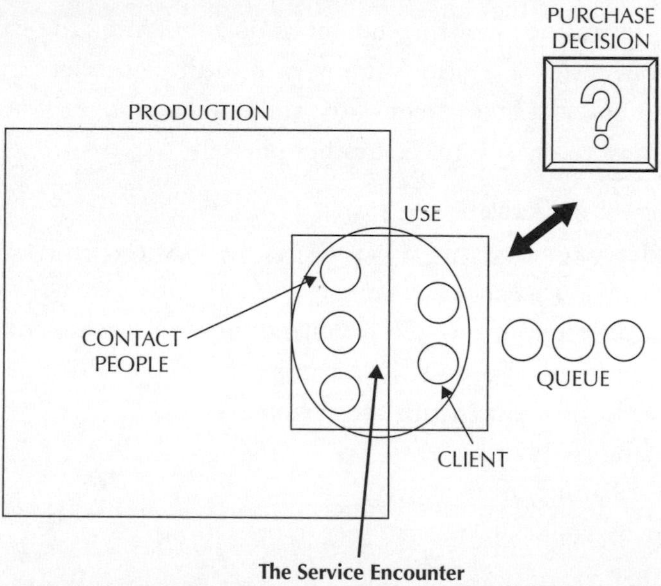

Source: "Arrow Guide—Increasing Satisfaction of Service Customers," The Arrow Group, Ltd.®, New York, 2008. Used with permission.

Exhibit 5.2 The Product Business System

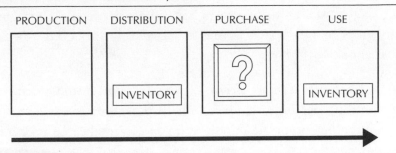

Source: "Arrow Guide—Increasing Satisfaction of Service Customers," The Arrow Group, Ltd.®, New York, 2008. Used with permission.

(see Exhibit 5.2). Instead, the products are distributed to the customer—sometimes through several levels. Anyone in the distribution channel can inventory the products, including the customer, so there is a buffer between production of the product and demand for the product—unlike services where the service is consumed as it is produced.

For products, the attributes of the brand must be clearly and consistently associated with the brand identifiers such as the brand name or brand logo so that the brand attributes move with the product through the distribution system. Because products were being transported and sold far away from where they were manufactured after the Industrial Revolution, brands emerged so that consumers and customers could identify the products with particular attributes.

Associations between the brand and its attributes must be developed for services just as for products but, in addition, the desired brand attributes must be clearly and consistently supported by each and every contact between your customer contact employees and your customers. That means all your service employees must understand what the brand stands for and why the brand is important:

> **The desired service brand attributes must be clearly and consistently supported by each and every contact between your customer contact employees and your customers.**

Such ongoing support may also be required at times with products as there may be substantial interpersonal contact between the producers, distributors, and customers as the product travels through the distribution channel.

Role of Customer Contact People in Creating the Brand Being the organization's person in contact with customers can be a tough job. You are the person in the middle and you can get beaten up a lot by unhappy customers. That means your customer contact people need to be recruited specially and trained, managed, and motivated specially (see Chapter 23 for more on this). One danger of the customer contact person being in the middle is that they may become more a representative of the customer than of the company. Training must stress the need to *professionalize contacts* with the customer without losing personal concern and empathy.

Taco Bell, the large fast-food provider, tries to find people who have a service mentality—a willingness to help customers. They feel it is easier to teach someone how to build a taco than it is to teach them how to relate to a customer. In Australia, Sanity Music, a music retailer, credited their growth in market share to the enthusiasm and knowledge of the salespeople they recruited.

Southwest Airlines spends well-above the airline industry average on training their customer contact people and it pays back. Southwest routinely is rated among the highest service companies in the United States as regards courtesy and helpfulness of their employees. Southwest also benefits from being able to choose from more than 30 applicants for every position.

Those who serve the customers need to be *empowered* so that they are satisfied in their jobs. For example, after increasing the power of their customer servers to handle customer complaints, American Express found employee turnover dropped 30 percent in three months. In general, organizations such as Sears and Marriott have found improvement in service employee morale and consequent decreases in employee turnover to be important determinants of increases in customer retention and in revenues.

Your employees who interact with your customers must be *informed* as to what your brand stands for and why the brand—and their actions to support the brand—are crucial to your organization. Studies by the Conference Board ("Managing the Corporate Brand," New York, 1998) and by the American Productivity and Quality Center ("Brand Building and Communication," Houston, 1999) have found that one of the characteristics of organizations that manage brands well is that their employees fully understand the brand strategy and the need for a brand strategy.

The slogan of the Chinese immigration service is clearly posted in mainland Chinese airports: "We hope to supply the most satisfactory service for you!" The importance of fulfilling the slogan is very clearly communicated to the immigration officers. At each cubicle where an immigration officer sits is a small electronic device that allows the traveler to rate immediately the service of the officer from "Greatly satisfied" to "Dissatisfied" by pushing the appropriate button.

Informing your employees of your brand strategy can be done in several ways such as meetings, messages, and a brand book (explaining the brand) and backed up by including good brand behavior as part of a reward system. When I helped a utility company develop their brand strategy, I was asked to provide presentations to all their service people so they would understand what the brand stood for and why that was important to the success of the company. Chapter 23 discusses at length how to ensure your employees support your brand.

EMPLOYEES OF THE TRUMP HOTEL COLLECTION

The Trump Hotel Collection believes that great service starts with the employees: Hire the best and make them feel special. Provide them an environment that is both challenging and nurturing.

Trump service is based on the following principle: "Our guests expect perfection—we must deliver." Employees are

---

(continued)

Lobby of Trump International Hotel & Tower New York
Photo courtesy of the Trump Organization.

expected to perform according to Donald Trump's pillars of success: passion, drive, and enthusiasm.

During their orientation, new employees of Trump hotels learn the Trump service standards and their role in providing such a level of service. Their internal goal is unparalleled service for the guests, with an objective of securing 100 percent loyalty.

Emphasis is placed on the responsibility of the associates to recognize when a guest is upset and to make things right. Associates are recognized for coming up with their own solutions for guest issues but also understand what they are allowed to do in any situation. Complaints and how they are resolved are tracked.

Associates do not interact with guests until they have completed a training program and have been approved by the trainer.

Source: Trump Hotel Collection internal document, April 23, 2007.

Service Environment and Process

While the customer contact person is very important, the success of the service encounter and the brand also depends on the *service environment* and what are called the peripherals—products used during the service. Benetton and Diesel, among many other retailers, carefully design their store interiors to please their target customers and reinforce their brand attributes of style.

Airlines spend a lot of money determining the color schemes for the interiors of aircraft. Similarly, dentists and physicians need to think about the ambience of their waiting rooms. Certainly medical professionals consider the décor of their offices and examination rooms where typically they display all their diplomas and awards—an important way to communicate their expertise to their patients. As regards peripherals, restaurants choose their dishes and flatware to be consistent with their brand positioning.

The *service process* needs to be organized for the benefit of the customers or clients. Many companies that employ an automated customer response (ACR) system to respond to telephone calls do not seem to understand that the process should be set up for the customers' convenience, not simply to save the company money. The ACR system for one large insurance company, for example, requires answers to several questions before allowing the customer to enter their identification number and then proceeds to provide lists of options of interest to few customers—the process is totally at odds with their avowed brand position of "caring" about their policyholders. In contrast, some organizations, such as Citibank, allow you to contact a customer service representative early in the ACR process, rather than forcing you through numerous agonizing options.

Intangibility of Benefits

Services need to be experienced to be evaluated. That means services are intangible as compared to products. The intangibility of services affects how you can present and communicate your brand.

Because they are intangible, the *search process* is more difficult for potential customers. For example, how would you go about finding a dentist in a strange city?

If you are marketing services, many of your customers may appreciate knowing the criteria they should use to evaluate services—such as universities, hospitals, or attorneys. That helps them structure their decisions and builds their confidence to make a choice. It is also an opportunity for you to manage your brand by spotlighting those attributes on which your brand performs well. For example, if you are a hospital administrator, you may advise prospective patents to choose a hospital on the basis of the experience of the surgeons and then mention the substantial experience of the surgeons associated with your institution—perhaps your key brand attribute.

Service organizations need to think of ways they can offer *trial experiences* to prospective customers. While that may be difficult for a surgeon, it is possible for a health club to provide potential customers with sample classes or for a hotel to provide a night or two "on the house." That allows prospective members to experience the brand firsthand.

Customers shopping for services need to *rely more on others' experiences* with the service because they may not be able to view it before purchase. Brand communications can make the benefits of the service clear to the client. That can be done with testimonials, demonstrations, or other messages that show the service experience, such as ads from MetLife. For some services, the Internet can be used to provide virtual experiences. For example, Hilton Worldwide Resorts, an upscale hotel chain, offers 360-degree online virtual walkthroughs of their rooms and facilities, as well as downloadable brochures and welcome packs ("Hilton Offers Virtual Tours to Drive Sales," *Precision Marketing*, April 30, 2004, p. 5).

Before the customers purchase, service providers should *manage their expectations* to manage their perceptions of the brand. At the start of any course, an effective professor makes very clear to the students what the course covers and how it will be covered. Similarly, a lawyer involved in drawing up a contract outlines what the process will be like and what possible outcomes might be expected.

MetLife Financial Services advertisement.

Perishability of Benefits

Because services are typically consumed when they are sold, there is usually *no inventory* in service organizations. No inventory means that capacity planning and demand management are especially important to service organizations and may affect how customers perceive the brand's position.

Capacity planning concerns how many service employees and how much equipment you need during a day or during a week. That requires *demand forecasting*. For example, capacity planning for airlines is very complicated. Universities face similar issues in scheduling courses.

Demand can be managed with communications and with pricing. Hotels that cater to business travelers during the week offer special discounts for couples and families on weekends so that they can better utilize their rooms. Utility companies offer special rates for power usage during the night so they can spread their demand more evenly.

Perishability of the service means that *timeliness* is often an important brand benefit to the customer or client. Continental Airlines and Southwest Airlines make punctuality an important part of their brand positioning.

Involvement of Customer in Operations

Patrons in a restaurant, students in a university, passengers on an airline, and guests at a resort all are involved in the delivery of the service. If they are not informed as to how to behave, then that may have a negative impact on the service experience for everyone around them and that will affect the brand.

Supporting the brand may mean that your customer contact people need to be *educators*—showing or explaining customers how to behave. Airlines do some education formally, at the start of each flight, when attendants explain the safety procedures and when they also describe the classes of service on the flight. Movie theaters usually caution audience members to turn off their cell telephones so as not to annoy others. Professors and other speakers provide a similar warning.

Educating customers requires customer contact people who are tolerant, patient, and courteous—again part of the training or advice they need to receive.

Customer education is easier the simpler the *service process* is. That is why hospitals try to streamline the admission process for their patients—for the sake of efficiency for both the patients and for the hospital staff. Internet travel services such as Expedia and Travelocity constantly strive to make their online reservation processes simpler to use and consequently easier to understand.

Because service customers may be part of the production process, they may identify with the service organization. That is good as regards building brand loyalty. However, it can also create an *inertia* that makes it difficult for the organization to reposition its brand by changing its processes or services. For example, if a government agency such as a post office or a motor vehicle department has long done certain things in a certain way, change may be opposed by customers who are used to the old way and do not see any reason for the new way. I worked with the Metropolitan Opera in New York on their marketing and we found that some of their most loyal supporters were sometimes the most difficult to persuade when a change was proposed.

Of course, in such circumstances, you have to carefully explain and show why change is needed—in terms of how the new system benefits the customer. If you cannot persuade the customers of why the new system is better, you will have difficulty changing the brand position.

Conclusion

Services pose special branding challenges due to their special characteristics. For service organizations, the perception of the brand often depends on the service encounter that depends on the skills and personalities of the people involved. In addition, due to issues such as intangibility, brand communications for services, including customer education and demand management, require special attention.

II

MANAGING THE BRAND

6

DEVELOPING A BRAND
STRATEGY FOR ANYTHING

The brand strategy is the foundation of your brand activities. Without a brand strategy, there are no guidelines for what you do or what your colleagues and employees do as regards the brand. Without a brand strategy, brand actions are aimless.

The brand strategy describes the desired brand position which, when supported by the marketing programs, results in the achievement of the business objectives.

In this chapter, you learn the main purposes of a strategy and how to develop a brand strategy that will be effective in achieving your objectives.

TRUMP HOME® FURNITURE

Strategy for Trump Home® furniture is a classic brand strategy based on an existing brand.

The Trump Home® brand includes two collections of furniture—Westchester™ which is more traditional and Central Park™ which is more contemporary. Both collections were inspired by the various properties owned by Donald Trump, including Mar-a-Lago and Trump Towers. Each collection was designed to provide a specific type of experience—a luxury manor or a luxury penthouse. The partner is Lexington Home Brands.

Trump Home® Furniture

The target audience consists of men and women, ages 25 to 50, who "want a luxury lifestyle with a touch of flair at an attainable price." The lines are not designed to be masculine or feminine. Target decision-makers include both men and women although frequently wives appear to play a key role in deciding on furniture. The collections were designed to create a home "that represents their preferred lifestyle for their families . . . one that represents [the wife's] dreams for the family."

Donald Trump describes the positioning of "the Trump Home® lifestyle [as] affordable luxury that has a look of success and status. [The] collection is absolute proof that you can live richly without spending a fortune."

Communications programs include dealer advertising and in-store promotions as well as advertising in home publications.

Source: Jo Fleischer, "Household Name Donald Trump," *Home Furnishings Business,* March 26, 2007; "The Donald Was Ready to Dance with Lexington," *Furniture Today,* March 26, 2007, pp. 4, 182; and "Lexington's Haney Shares Insights on Trump Line," *Furniture Today,* March 26, 2007, p. 182.

THE THREE MAIN PURPOSES OF A BRAND STRATEGY

Your brand strategy should accomplish three objectives:

1. *Coordinate* all the functions of your organization so that they are all working together to create and maintain a strong brand.
2. *Concentrate* your resources so that they are used most effectively.
3. *Communicate* to those involved with the brand—usually nearly everyone in the organization—what they must do to create and maintain a strong brand.

Coordinate

Think of an organization in terms of its various functional areas: finance, sales, operations, human resources, research and development, legal.

Let's focus on three of those functions: sales, operations, and finance (see Exhibit 6.1).

Suppose you were head of sales and the CEO of your organization told you: "You can have anything you want to help you increase unit sales. No problem with budget. Just tell me what you want." After you picked yourself up from the floor where you had fallen in surprise, you might answer: "Many more salespeople. Highest salaries. Substantial commissions and bonuses. Lots of training. Many versions of the product or service. Easy credit. Low prices. Lots of advertising. Fine automobiles for the salespeople. Lavish expense budgets. Frequent sales contests with attractive prizes."

Suppose you were head of operations and the CEO of your organization told you: "You can have anything you want to help you produce more units." You might answer: "Many more operations personnel. Highest salaries. New, large facilities. Large raw material inventories. One version of the product or service. No advertising. Appropriate (flexible) quality control."

And, if you were head of finance and the CEO of your organization asked you to control expenses, you might simply say "No" to the expenditures for all these sales and operations initiatives.

Exhibit 6.1 Brand Strategy Coordinates Functions

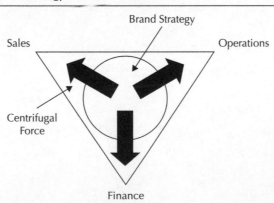

Source: "Arrow Guide—Formulating the Product/Market Strategy," The Arrow Group, Ltd.®, New York, 2008. Used with permission.

In many organizations, there are centrifugal forces—often related to the various functions of the organization—that pull the organization in different ways. A strategy is needed to *coordinate* those functions. There are times when you want many versions of the product. There are times when you want one version of the product. And there are times you need to say no. Without a strategy, these centrifugal forces can paralyze an organization. Your strategy provides the theme that ensures the various functions are pulling in the same direction.

Consider a restaurant. The chef may want to attempt esoteric new dishes. The wait staff may want to be casual in their dress and grooming and informal with the clientele. The owner may want to provide a luxurious experience for the restaurant's patrons. Unless they all agree on the brand position for the restaurant, branding chaos may result.

Concentrate

A well-known military maxim is:

Concentrate your firepower.

The same maxim is true for branding. If there are too many customer targets for your branding efforts, two problems arise. First, your scarce resources—everyone's resources are scarce—may be spread too thin to have any impact. Second, your brand image may be blurred if the brand is positioned somewhat differently for each customer target. Strong brands are built with consistency and too many targets can make consistency difficult to achieve.

To concentrate your branding efforts requires understanding of the customers or consumers in your market. If you manage a contracting business, for example, you need to know which customers require a full range of services from you and which customers require only some of your services because they are capable of doing some work themselves. How you might develop your brand would likely differ depending on which set of customers you target. For those without expertise, you might tout your ability to do everything for them without their need to supervise. For those with expertise, you might exploit your experience that can supplement and support their own abilities.

Concentrating branding efforts also requires the ability to say "No." If you have never said "No" to a customer, then you probably don't have a brand strategy. There are many customers you want but there are some that you do not want because they will not be as profitable for you as other customers and catering to them will use resources that you could use to serve your more profitable customers.

If you think everyone is your customer, then no one is your customer.

Communicate

Studies by the Conference Board ("Managing the Corporate Brand," New York, 1998) and the American Productivity and Quality Center ("Brand Building and Communication," Houston, 1999) have found that employee understanding of the brand and employee involvement in the brand are key factors in building and managing a successful brand. If employees do not know what the desired brand position is, it will be difficult for them to act in ways that support the brand.

Have you ever had a *telepathic* manager? A manager who thinks they are telepathic is someone who does not say what she or he expects you to do but nonetheless expects you somehow to read their mind so that you will do what they want. Research and common sense suggest that if you want someone to do something, you need to tell them.

The brand strategy—especially the brand position—must be communicated throughout the organization. Ways to make clear the brand strategy to your employees are discussed in the final chapter, Chapter 23, "Your Employees and Your Brand."

Components of the Brand Strategy

A brand strategy consists of four major parts (see Exhibit 6.2):

1. *Target market:* The customers or consumers on which efforts will be focused
2. *Business objectives:* The financial goals such as revenue or profits over time
3. *Brand positioning:* The key benefits that are the reasons customers or consumers make the purchase
4. *Programs:* The actions you take including tactics such as advertising, promotion, and pricing that are used to implement the strategy

Exhibit 6.2   Components of a Brand Strategy*

	TIME PERIOD	1	2	3	4
Target Market	Which customers do you want?				
Business Objectives	What do you want from the business?				
Target DMU Member	To whom specifically must you communicate?				
Target Competitor	What competitor do you need to defeat?				
Benefit Advantage	Why should customers buy from you?				
Competitive Advantage	Why will you win?				
Branding Programs: Identifiers Advertising Promotion Public Relations Selling Internet Other	How will you implement your branding strategy?				

Brand Positioning brackets the rows from Target DMU Member through Competitive Advantage.

DMU = Decision-making unit.

Source: "Arrow Guide—Guerrilla Branding," The Arrow Group, Ltd.®, New York, 2008. Used with permission. **A blank version of this page can be downloaded from www.trumpuniversity.com/ branding101 and customized for your personal use.* For any other use, contact Don Sexton at Branding101@thearrowgroup.com.

Of these components, the choice of target market and brand positioning are *strategic choices*. They have a major impact on the success of your organization. The programs represent *tactical choices*. Tactics are important but if the target market and brand positioning are incorrect, generally tactics alone cannot lead to successful performance. (Key brand programs or tactics are discussed in Chapters 7 and 8.)

Suppose you are taking an airplane trip. The strategic choices of your brand strategy would be analogous to your destination—the city you are planning to visit. The tactical choices of your brand strategy are analogous to where you sit in the aircraft. Suppose somehow you were able to go out on the tarmac and enter an aircraft. Inside, suppose you found your ideal seat—aisle with lots of leg room. Your tactics would be optimal but suppose you wanted to go to Detroit and that particular plane was going to Seattle. Your strategy would not be successful despite your optimal tactics. Before you get on the airplane and select a seat, you need to be sure it is going where you want to go. Before you develop brand programs, you need to be clear of your target market and positioning.

LEVELS OF BRAND STRATEGY

Brand strategies can be constructed at several levels (see Exhibit 6.3). The overall brand structure in an organization is known as the *brand architecture* (see Chapter 9).

The associations of corporate brands should summarize the brand position of the entire organization. For example, reliability for FedEx or innovation for 3M. As you move down in level, the brand position should be more specific—for a strategic business unit or a group of products or services. Brands for specific products or services are usually known as *subbrands* and communicate the key benefits for those products or services. If there are multiple versions of those products or services, such as different flavors of breakfast cereals, then there would be modifiers for the product or service brand.

Exhibit 6.3 Levels of Brand Strategies

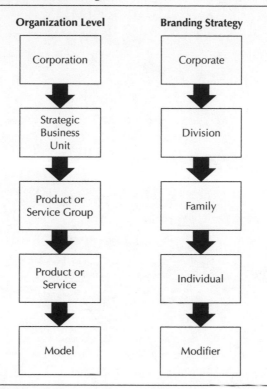

Source: "Arrow Guide—Formulating the Brand Strategy," The Arrow Group, Ltd.®, New York, 2008. Used with permission.

Organizations may build their brands at any level. Corporate brands offer efficiency—one brand covering many products or services. However, corporate brands need to have positions sufficiently broad to cover the positions of all the products and services in an organization's portfolio. For a company like GE, there may be many products and services such as aircraft engines, plastics, medical equipment, and financial services; to find a corporate brand position in which they all fit comfortably can be a difficult task.

Building brands at the product or service level provides the opportunity to communicate a very specific brand position. The drawback is that each branded product or service must have sales sufficient to justify a separate brand.

3M advertisements showing brand architecture.

There is no "right" level at which to develop a brand strategy. For some companies such as GE and IBM, most of their brand equity probably is at the corporate brand level. For other companies such as Procter & Gamble and Unilever, most of their brand equity is likely at the product or service level.

Often the levels of brand strategy depend as much on historical chance than on strategic thinking. If you were building a brand architecture from scratch, you might want to consider a two-level branding architecture. The corporate brand would be connected to the market life cycle or the market need. The product or service brands would be connected to the particular benefits of the product or service. For example, in men's shaving products, Gillette (now part of Procter & Gamble) developed their corporate brand to stand for "the best a man can get" while their subbrands (such as Sensor and Mach-3) stood for benefits related to specific technologies.

Marriott has been organized by markets and types of hotels. The full-service group of hotels included the Marriott, Renaissance Hotels and Resorts, and Marriott Conference Center brands. The select service brands included Courtyard, Spring Hill Suites, and Fairfield Inn. The extended stay brands included Residence Inn and ExecuStay. The Ritz-Carlton operations were managed separately (Mike Beirne, "Marriott Tiers Its Brands to Propel Chain Growth," *Adweek*, November 22, 1999; and Edwin McDowell, "Greater Than the Sum of Its Parts," *New York Times*, November 29, 1996, p. D-9). Such an organization structure allows managers freedom to focus their brand strategies.

STEPS IN CONSTRUCTING THE BRAND STRATEGY

There are four main steps in constructing the brand strategy. Detailed descriptions of each of these steps can be found in the companion book, *Trump University Marketing 101* (Hoboken, NJ: Wiley, 2006):

1. Situation analysis
2. Market segmentation
3. Assembly of the strategy
4. Forecasting results

Situation Analysis

During the situation analysis, you immerse yourself in all the information available on your competitive situation. You consider your possible customers and what might be their needs. You identify possible competitors and predict their likely actions. You evaluate your organization with respect to its capabilities. You explore macro changes such as demographic, technological, economic, social, or political trends that might affect you and the performance of your brand strategy.

Situation analysis consists of a lot of time spent reviewing information—studies, plans, analyses—and talking to people experienced with your market. It may amount to more than half of the time spent constructing the brand strategy but your conclusions form the foundation of your branding strategy.

Market Segmentation

The first part of market segmentation consists of *identifying* possible market segments. The second part is *selecting* those segments on which you wish to focus your branding efforts.

You target market segments so you can concentrate your efforts on groups of customers who are similar as regards what they want from your product or service. David Sibley, MTV Europe's general manager and senior vice-president of international marketing partnerships, described the central role of their target market in their branding activities: "We stay true to our core demographic of 16- to 35-year-olds, so we extend our brand where we feel it's relevant and entertaining [to them]" ("The Brand Stretchers," *Campaign*, September 24, 2004, p. 29).

A *market segment* is a group of customers or potential customers who have a similar problem *or* seek approximately the same benefits.

The word *problem* refers to the customer's needs. Typically, that problem can be characterized in terms of benefits sought—the dimensions of the customer's problem. For example, an airline passenger may be concerned with arriving at his destination on time or the client of an accountant may want to be sure that her taxes are done accurately but with as much savings as possible. Generally, you will position your product or service differently for different segments—if the positions are the same, then the segments are the same. For example, the Bahamas brand was positioned differently for families versus for young couples.

When you are identifying and selecting market segments, always remember that the information must come from the customers,

Bahamas advertisements for different market segments.

consumers, or clients. Although you may have a lot of experience with customers, it is important to use information from them whenever possible.

Market Segmentation—Realty Example Suppose you have a small real estate agency. Possible segments might include singles, young couples, young families, mature families, and empty nesters (older couples whose children have left home).

To determine if these segments are in fact distinct market segments, you need to consider the benefits that real estate customers might seek such as financing expertise, knowledge of area schools, accessibility of realtor, and realtor's ability to match homes with the customers' needs. You also would want to estimate how important these benefits are to members in each group, perhaps on a 1 to 10 scale where 10 means "very important."

You can arrange all this information in a Segment Identification Chart (see Exhibit 6.4).

Exhibit 6.4   Segment Identification Chart with Real Estate Segments*

Benefits	Descriptors of possible segments				
	Singles	Young Couples	Young Families	Mature Families	Empty Nesters
FINANCING EXPERTISE	7	10	10	6	6
RENTAL EXPERTISE	10	7	5	2	8
SMALL HOME EXPERTISE	8	9	9	1	9
LARGE HOME EXPERTISE	1	3	2	9	1
SCHOOL EXPERTISE	2	5	9	7	1
MATCH HOMES WITH NEEDS	7	8	8	6	7
UNDERSTANDING OF NEEDS	8	6	8	7	9

10 = Very important; 1 = Not important.

Source: "Arrow Guide—Segment Identification Analysis," The Arrow Group®, New York, 2008. Used with permission. ***A blank version of this page can be downloaded from www .trumpuniversity.com/branding101 and customized for your personal use.** For any other use, contact Don Sexton at Branding101@thearrowgroup.com.

Exhibit 6.4 shows that singles may be especially concerned with how well the realtor knows the rental market while young families may be interested particularly in financing expertise and knowledge of school systems. As regards benefits and priorities, some segments may resemble others. For example, in Exhibit 6.4 singles and empty nesters value similar benefits.

If segment members are similar, you may be able to combine them into one segment in terms of determining brand position although you still may need to communicate to them differently—singles will likely be listening to different radio stations than seniors.

Once you have identified possible segments, you can then systematically evaluate them to determine on which ones you will concentrate your branding efforts. List the market segments you are considering and then evaluate each one on two dimensions: how attractive the segment would be to you and your relative ability to win customers from that segment.

In the real estate example, suppose young couples, young families, and perhaps empty nesters would likely be attractive market segments for you because of the sizes of their markets. Mature families—families with pre-college-age children—might also be attractive because of the larger homes they might buy. Singles might be less attractive segments because they would likely prefer rentals or smaller homes. Use a five-point scale to rate attractiveness for each segment where 5 means "very attractive" and 1 means "not attractive."

Suppose that your real estate office rates high on expertise regarding small homes. That would give you relatively high ability to sell to young couples, young families, and empty nesters. Knowing less about larger homes might be a disadvantage with customers in the mature family segment and so your relative ability would be rated lower for that segment.

Use a five-point scale to rate relative ability where 5 means "high relative ability" and 1 means "low relative ability."

These evaluations of attractiveness and relative ability allow you to plot the different segments in the *Segment Selection Chart* (Exhibit 6.5). Those market segments of highest promise to you are in the upper left quadrant—high attractiveness and high relative ability. You will probably want to focus your branding efforts on market segments from that quadrant. However, do not ignore the segments in the upper right quadrant—some of them may have long-term potential and are worth considering. Also, do not ignore any segments in the lower left quadrant—they often represent your current customer base and you do not want to forget about them. Market segments in the lower right quadrant—low attractiveness and low relative ability—usually are not segments on which you want to expend much effort (although occasionally there may be exceptions).

Exhibit 6.5   Segment Selection Chart with Real Estate Segments*

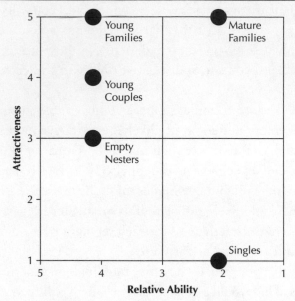

Attractiveness: 1=Not attractive; 5=Very attractive.
Relative ability: 1=Weak; 5=Strong.

Source: "Arrow Guide—Segment Selection Chart," The Arrow Group®, New York, 2008. Used with permission. ***A blank version of this page can be downloaded from www .trumpuniversity.com/branding101 and customized for your personal use.** For any other use, contact Don Sexton at Branding101@thearrowgroup.com.

Overall, be very careful that you do not attempt too much by going after every segment. If you are focusing on all customers, then you are really focusing on no customers at all. Concentrating on too many distinct segments can deplete your resources and blur your brand.

Positioning

Positioning is the heart of the brand strategy. Positioning is the theme that orchestrates all your branding programs.

Positioning consists of one, two, or perhaps three benefits that customers want and that you can provide at a level superior to what your competitors can do.

To determine your positioning involves four questions:

1. To whom specifically must you communicate? This is the target member of the decision-making unit (DMU; all those involved in making the buying decision). For example, a roof contractor might emphasize durability to one spouse and aesthetics to another. The contractor's positioning depends on which spouse they wish to focus their efforts.

   Many branding or marketing books do not include a target DMU member in their definition of positioning. Instead, they define positioning in relation to an entire market segment. As any salesperson knows, that is a mistake. Selling is done person-to-person, not person-to-segment. You need to think of the *individual* you wish to target whenever you are developing a position for your brand.

2. What competitor do you need to defeat? There are always competitors; however, sometimes you can choose which ones you fight. They are your target competitors. You would like to fight against significant competitors you know you can defeat. You may know you can keep your food store open longer than the local supermarket and win those customers for whom time convenience is a key benefit.

3. Why should customers buy from you? This idea is so important in marketing that it has been given many different names such as *point of difference*, *unique selling proposition*, and *differential advantage*. I call it your *benefit advantage*.

   Your benefit advantage should be the one or two—at most three—benefits that you will emphasize and communicate to your target customers. These benefits must be benefits your

85

target customers care about and they must be benefits that you provide more successfully than your competitors. The hardware store that provides do-it-yourself advice. The beauty salon that provides tanning services. The soap that provides a pleasant aroma.

For example, suppose you open a service advising businesses regarding their computer use. Do you want to be known for the breadth of your expertise, for the speed with which you respond, for your courtesy, or for your around-the-clock availability? Even if you do all of these well, you may want to concentrate your communications on just one so that you occupy a clearer position in your customer's mind.

4. Why will you win? For a business to succeed in the long run, it must have capabilities that its competitors do not have. This is known as the business' *competitive advantage*. Competitive advantages may be due to people—a restaurant with a gifted chef—or resources—a retail store with a convenient location. Successful businesses typically have one or more capabilities that allow them to satisfy their target customers more effectively or more efficiently than their target competitors.

Your competitive advantage is your capability that—because it is superior to that of your target competitor's—allows your benefit advantage to be sustainable. A competitive advantage may be a skill associated with people, a resource, or a feature of your product or service. For example, a hardware store may be able to provide do-it-yourself advice because their floor staff has the knowledge and the time to talk with customers. The beauty salon may provide tanning services since they have the necessary equipment. The soap may have a pleasant aroma because of special ingredients.

Determining the Brand Position   Branding requires discipline and that starts with determining your brand position. You want to have a clear position understood by your customers. You want to be the automobile dealer with the most courteous and knowledgeable sales staff, the

Building a Powerful Brand Strategy: Miller Lite

Was Miller Lite the first low-calorie beer in the United States?

In 1966, six years before the introduction of Miller Lite in 1972 the first low-calorie beer in the United States was introduced—Gablinger's Beer. Their first print ad touted Gablinger's as "Great tasting premium beer 100 percent fat free, less calories than skim milk."

Gablinger's beer was targeted for dieters but, if you are dieting, you don't drink any beer because low-calorie beers have only one-third fewer calories. Gablinger's did not do well.

The genius of the Miller Lite brand strategy was to avoid the obvious diet position and stake out another position. What do you think of when you hear "Miller Lite"? Tastes great? Less filling? Notice that those are two benefits. When you put them together, you get a different kind of a benefit. "Tastes great, less filling" translates to "Now you can drink as much as you want and you won't feel filled up." Miller Lite did not go after dieters but the opposite—people who like to drink a lot of beer.

Gablinger's advertisement and Miller Lite advertisement.

(continued)

In 1972, Miller Brewing was number seven among brewers in the United States. By 1979, they were number two. They jumped over everybody except Anheuser Busch. Eventually Anheuser Busch caught up when they came out with Bud Light. How did Miller Brewing succeed? The low-calorie beer segment that they developed took off with a growth rate of 35 percent a year while the beer market in general was growing only at about 5 percent a year.

realtor with the most geographical expertise, or the health club with the greatest variety of equipment.

Brands help sustain your benefit advantage. However, when choosing a benefit advantage, when possible choose one that can be sustained due to your capabilities. Such a benefit will add strength to the brand. For example, if you are an accountant focusing on owners of small apartment buildings, be sure you are and remain the expert in tax laws and regulations governing the operation of such buildings.

Positioning—Realty Example Suppose you owned a small realty firm that specialized in the senior couples market. Exhibit 6.6 shows how you might position your business. Your target customer might be the husband or wife and your target competitor national realty chains. Perhaps your target customers are older couples whose children have left home and who are now looking to move from a large home to a small home or condominium. They would value agents who possessed expertise concerning small homes or condominiums and who understand their concerns and needs. Suppose you employed agents with such expertise who also happened to be in the same generation so understood the seniors' viewpoint. Your agents would be your competitive advantage who would provide your benefit advantages of expertise and understanding. Those benefit advantages should be the attributes you connect to the brand of your realty business.

Exhibit 6.6   Positioning Description—Real Estate Example*

Product or Service: Real estate Target Market Segment: Empty Nesters—Older Couples without Children	
Target Member of Decision-Making Unit	Wife and Husband
Target Competitor	Chain Realtor
Benefit Advantages	Expertise for Small Homes or Rentals Understanding of Older Couples' Concerns
Competitive Advantages	Knowledge of Local Retirement Developments Mature Agents

Source: "Arrow Guide—Formulating the Brand Strategy," The Arrow Group, Ltd.®, New York, 2008. Used with permission. ***A blank version of this page can be downloaded from www .trumpuniversity.com/branding101 and customized for your personal use.*** For any other use, contact Don Sexton at Branding101@thearrowgroup.com.

In this example, relevant expertise and understanding were important and were benefits your agents could provide.

"There never was a plan."
Illustration courtesy of Ashleigh Brilliant, © 2008 Ashleigh Brilliant.

Conclusion

Brand strategies coordinate your activities, concentrate your efforts, and communicate to your people what they must do to support your brand. A brand strategy describes what must be done to achieve your business objectives. Central to an effective brand strategy are the choices of target market and brand positioning. Brand programs support the brand and implement the brand strategy.

7

TELLING PEOPLE ABOUT
YOUR BRAND

Y ou need a great strategy to build your brand, but to make it happen you also need strong execution of all your branding communications. Your target market and brand positioning define your strategy
but your strategy is implemented with your brand communications.

Even though your product or service meets the needs of your target customers better than any other brand, purchases will not take
place until your customer agrees that your product or service meets
their needs better. Your brand communications must convincingly
convey your brand position.

In this chapter, you learn the principles for developing an effective
brand communications program.

TRUMP HOME® LIGHTING

The Trump Organization partnered with ELK Lighting to produce
Trump Home® branded lighting, which complements the Trump
Home® furniture and Trump Home® floor coverings. The

(continued)

Westchester™ collection is "grand, classic styling" in the spirit of country mansions while the Central Park™ collection is more contemporary.

Trump Home Lighting®
Photos courtesy of the Trump Organization.

Bradford Smith, CEO of ELK Lighting, believes, "Lighting should be seen as 'jewelry' for the home and office. The use of lighting can enhance the mood and character."

The ELK Lighting design team attempts to capture the style and sophistication associated with the Donald J. Trump brand.

Communications are varied and include print and broadcast media. In addition, Donald Trump has indicated that, "We are exploring opportunities to include Trump Home® [products] in many of our Trump properties."

Source: Nancy Meyer, *HFN,* June 11, 2007, p. 28; and "Donald J. Trump & ELK Lighting to Launch Trump Branded Residential Lighting Line," The Trump Organization press release, October 10, 2006.

WHAT TO COMMUNICATE?

Once you have determined your brand position, you need to consider whether your target customers agree with you—whether their perceptions of the brand are what you want.

You are looking for *gaps* between what you want your brand position to be and what your customers think it is. If there are gaps between their perceptions and your desired brand position on certain key attributes, then you need to move to close those gaps with your brand communications.

You need to find the gaps between your brand position and your customers' perceptions.

You can find these gaps by talking to your customers or potential customers. First you need to know what attributes are the most important to them. Then for those attributes in particular you want to know what they think of your brand.

Suppose you operate a Laundromat and suppose that you know, from conversations with customers, that not having to wait for washers or dryers and cleanliness of the space are the most important benefits to your target customers. You have spent a lot of money to purchase the most reliable machines and you have them serviced regularly so they are always running. You also employ someone to mop the floor, empty trash, replace light bulbs, and otherwise keep the space looking clean. In fact, you believe you are much better at both of these attributes than any of your nearby competitors.

However, your customers must agree with your brand position before it will have any impact on your financial performance. If your customers do not believe that they will not have a long wait at your Laundromat or that the area is not sufficiently clean, then your brand position has not yet been established.

What you would need to do is develop a communications campaign to close the gaps between your customers' perceptions and your desired brand position. For example, you might use flyers to describe your new washers and dryers—better you might persuade some customers to provide testimonials that they never wait at your Laundromat and that the space is always spotless—so spotless that they let their babies play on the floor! (Well maybe you might not want to exaggerate that much.)

You can see this situation by sketching a perceptual map—as we explained in Chapter 4.

In Exhibit 7.1, the ideal point is the type of Laundromat your customers want. Hopefully that is the type of Laundromat you are providing—shown by the letter "A" for "Actual position" in the exhibit. "P" is your position as perceived by the customers. You need to let them know that you are providing them laundry services close to their ideal.

Exhibit 7.1 Perceptual Map: Laundromats

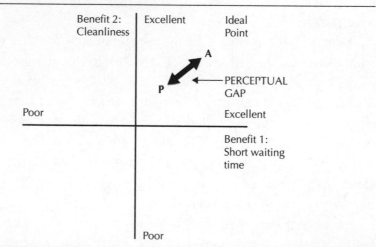

A = Actual position
P = Position perceived by customers
Ideal Point = Position customers want.

COMMUNICATIONS AND ACTIONS

It takes time to close perceptual gaps, which is one reason it takes time to build a brand position and perhaps even more time to change a brand position.

Why are you communicating your brand position to your target customer? To get them to take some action such as trying your product or buying it again or buying more. Your brand position is what should motivate them to behave in your favor—if you can successfully communicate it to them.

You communicate your brand position to your target customers so that they will ACT!

For a salesperson, one of the most frustrating situations is when they know they have a product or service that meets their customer's needs much better than do their competitors' products or services *but they can't talk to the customer because the customer is well-defended or is too satisfied to consider any other options.* That is the challenge of your brand communications—to develop a plan that will reach your customers through the clutter of information they receive and then persuade them to act.

PRINCIPLES OF BRAND COMMUNICATIONS

We know from communications research that you cannot expect a customer to change his or her mind about you immediately. Brand communications needs to be a series of nudges rather than a violent push. Thom McAn shoes were known for years as a sturdy, inexpensive shoe. They tried to change their humble but well-known position to a fashion-forward position in just a few months' time. In New York City, they tried to do that with subway advertisements such as the one in the photo. The ad declared that Thom McAn was a shoe fashion designer. Do you think I would believe some copywriter (who perhaps never wore Thom McAns) or my mother who bought me Thom McAn shoes every year while I was growing up? The campaign apparently failed and eventually the Thom McAn brand was acquired by Footstar, who are reviving it.

Brand communications need to address concerns of your customers to which they give high priority. If they do not consider an attribute important to them, they will very likely ignore your message entirely. Spectar is a plastic from Eastman Chemical—Spectar brand communications clearly show its key attribute of flexibility.

Thom McAn advertisement.

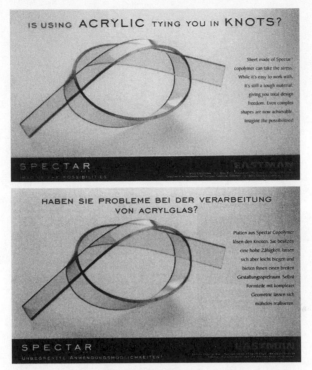

Spectar advertisements (United States and Germany).

Communications should be simple. Voted the most effective advertising campaign of all time was the DDB campaign introducing the Volkswagen "bug" to the United States in the 1950s. Each ad was very clean and typically focused on just one attribute of the automobile. Initially they used only print ads but these ads were so powerful that many people when asked about the VW ads said they loved the *television* ads.

Consistency in communications is what builds powerful brands. All your brand communications should reinforce each other.

Consistency in communications is what builds powerful brands.

Early Volkswagen advertisement.

How Communications Works

The key stages leading to purchase are often described as Awareness, Knowledge, Liking, Preference, Conviction, and Action (see Exhibit 7.2). This model is well-known in marketing and is called the *Hierarchy of Effects model* because it seems to describe the hierarchy of stages customers go through before purchase. Several people have been credited with suggesting this model.

Awareness is knowing the name of a brand. Knowledge consists of understanding the economic or functional benefits. Liking depends on

Exhibit 7.2   How Communications Works

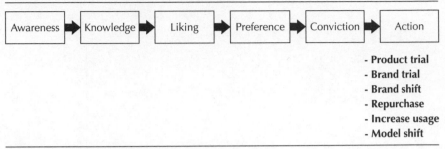

Awareness ➡ Knowledge ➡ Liking ➡ Preference ➡ Conviction ➡ Action

- Product trial
- Brand trial
- Brand shift
- Repurchase
- Increase usage
- Model shift

Source: "Arrow Guide—Managing Communications," The Arrow Group, Ltd.®, New York, 2008. Used with permission.

the emotional benefits. Preference means one brand is favored. Conviction is the decision to take action.

Action can mean purchasing the branded product for the first time (what is called a *trial*), repurchasing, purchasing more, or purchasing a more expensive version (e.g., a deluxe model automobile instead of the standard model). Each action requires somewhat different arguments to persuade the customer.

While the Hierarchy of Effects model has much superficial appeal, little research supports that it is true in every case. It does apply in certain situations but not in all situations. When building a brand, you must consider whether and how this model applies to your product or service.

In particular, the order of the stages of the cycle may well vary depending on the type of product or service. For example, for important purchases such as a home or most business-to-business purchases, there may be substantial information-gathering before purchase. However, for relatively less important purchases—including many consumer purchases such as a razor or a magazine, customers may simply make the purchase on a trial basis and do their information-gathering after the purchase.

When and how the Hierarchy of Effects model applies is shown in Exhibit 7.3. This grid is based on work at the advertising agency, Foote, Cone, and Belding. Purchase situations are classified according to how significant the purchase is and what types of brand attributes are most important—functional or emotional. The upper left corner is the situation

Exhibit 7.3 Types of Purchase Decisions

		Key Attributes	
		Functional	Emotional
Significance of Purchase	High Importance	LEARN/FEEL/DO	FEEL/LEARN/DO
	Low Importance	DO/LEARN/FEEL	DO/FEEL/LEARN

Adapted from Foot, Cone, and Belding, "New Insights about the FCB Grid," *Journal of Advertising Research,* August–September 1987.

when the Hierarchy of Effects model typically applies—important purchases where functional (or economic) attributes may determine the choice. For consumers, that would include many substantial purchases such as home computers and property for investment. Most business-to-business purchases also fall in this category. This case is known as "Learn/Feel/Do" because the customer first gains knowledge of the product, than may develop an emotional interest in the brand, and finally takes action.

The situation corresponding to the upper right corner also begins with "Learning." However, here the initial appeal concerns emotional aspects. Emotional attributes include excitement, style, and status but can also include reliability and security.

The customer may go on to consider functional attributes as well and then take action so this case is known as "Feel/Learn/Do." Note that the same product category may fall in either of these two corners. For an automobile used for basic transportation, functional benefits may have priority, while for an automobile for recreation, emotional benefits may be of more importance.

The two cases in the bottom row are for purchase situations where relatively little is at stake. In such circumstances, the customer may take action without much effort to investigate the product—simply try the product—and then base his or her evaluation mainly on firsthand experience. Such behavior may be visible for products where functional benefits are key such as batteries and razor blades and for products where emotional benefits are a main consideration such as men's ties and costume jewelry. Again, some product categories may be found in more than one situation. For example, athletic clothing may be evaluated on functional or emotional benefits and, depending on the dining situation, restaurants may be selected on functional or emotional benefits.

When you are designing your communications, keep in mind the type of purchase decision that your target customer may be making. If it is a choice with significant consequences such as where they may hold their wedding or what university they might attend, then you need to provide a lot of information early about why your brand is superior to those of your competitors. On the other hand, if it is a frequent purchase, then you do need to provide people with enough reason to try your product or service rather than that of another organization, but do not expect them to spend a lot of time mulling over the decision.

Using Nontraditional Brand Communications: BMW

In 1992, BMW introduced the Z3, a two-seater convertible, designed for several markets including young singles, fortyish men and women, and older drivers—all seeking a stylish, classic roadster. According to Jim McDowell, vice president of marketing, the communications goals included stimulating "the excitement and enthusiasm of the core customer base in a way that would draw broader attention and interest to the brand." Management referred to this as "leveraging the buzz."

To achieve this goal, BMW used both traditional and nontraditional communications. The nontraditional methods included

(continued)

BMW Z3 advertisement.

placing the product in a new James Bond film, *Golden Eye*. While the BMW Z3 appeared in the film for only about two minutes, it created considerable impact. BMW Z3's were lent to television hosts such as Jay Leno and radio personalities to use as they wished on their shows. The Z3 was offered in the Neiman-Marcus catalog. Dealers hosted parties for key customers where *Golden Eye* was prescreened. Meanwhile, these "buzz" efforts were reinforced by traditional print and television advertising.

BMW has continued to employ nontraditional communications. Other BMW products were placed in subsequent Bond films. Later, BMW sponsored a series of short films on the web, each featuring a BMW vehicle, the actor Clive Owen, and a well-known director such as Ang Lee and Guy Ritchie.

All these efforts helped BMW move from the clutter of traditional advertising and created substantial buzz for the brand at a manageable budget level.

Source: Conversations with B. Shetty, 1999, 2000, and J. McDowell, 1999; and material in L. Schmidt, "BMW Sizes Up the Cost of Luxury," *Business Review Weekly,* June 15, 1998; S. Fournier and R. J. Dolan, "Launching the BMW Z3 Roadster," 1997; and K. Kerwin, "BMW Could Use a Little Skid Control," *BusinessWeek,* January 24, 2000.

METHODS OF BRAND COMMUNICATIONS

There are numerous ways to communicate your brand position to members of your target market (see Exhibit 7.4).

- *Identifiers:* The identifiers consist of all the symbols that stand for your brand. That includes name, logo, shapes, aromas, colors—anything that would remind a customer of what your brand stands for.

Exhibit 7.4 Types of Media

Indentifiers	Advertising	Sales Promotion	Public Relations	Personal Selling
Packaging	Television	Couponing	Press Relations	Qualifying Customers
Brochures/ Manuals	Radio	Rebates	Product Publicity	Presentations
Décor (Atmospherics)	Print	Premiums		
Spokesperson	Cinema	Samples	Company Communications	Consultative Selling
Stationery	Outdoor	Contests	Donations/ Sponsorships	Entertainment
Signs				Trade Shows
Uniforms	Point of Purchase	Sweepstakes	Special Events	Telemarketing
Vehicles	Direct Mail	Trade Shows		
Website	Internet Advertising		Community Relations	
	Email		Lobbying	
	Web Site		Crisis Management	
	Blog			
	Nontraditional advertising			

Source: "Arrow Guide—Advertising Decisions," The Arrow Group, Ltd.®, New York, 2008. Used with permission.

- *Advertising:* Advertising comprises all the ways that organizations can pay for directing communications to customers. Traditional advertising includes broadcast media (television, radio), print media (magazines, newspapers), outdoor advertising, and the Internet. Nontraditional media include event sponsorship and product placements.
- *Sales promotion:* Sales promotion consists of providing an incentive to the customer—at any level in the distribution chain—to help persuade them to purchase. Incentives can be coupons, contests, and premiums.
- *Public relations:* Public relations makes use of unpaid media to communicate with customers. Public relations tools include press releases, speeches, events, and donations.
- *Personal selling:* For many products and services, personal selling is the main way the final sale is made. Many business products and services are sold through the efforts of sales representatives, also many consumer products—especially automobiles, consumer durables, such as large appliances, and certain financial products.

Detailed discussions of how to use each of these communications methods can be found in the companion book, *Trump University Marketing 101* (Hoboken, NJ: Wiley, 2006).

CONCLUSION

Building a brand requires consistent communications. The theme for your communications is provided by your brand positioning. The tone of your brand communications and the ways you contact your customers depend on your choice of target market. Without effective communications to your customers, your brand is just a good idea. Customers must agree with you about the desirability of your brand before they will purchase.

8

CHOOSING AND MANAGING
YOUR NAME AND LOGO

How many brand names can you see in this photo of the Shanghai waterfront?

Shanghai waterfront.
Photo credit: Don Sexton. Photo courtesy of Don Sexton.

Brand identifiers are the cues that lead the customer to associate attributes to your brand and are important components of the overall communications strategy for a brand. The brand identifiers are how your brand looks to the world.

In this chapter, you learn some of the important considerations in developing and managing your brand identifiers, especially your name and logo.

NAMING YOUR BRAND

Start with as many suggestions for the name as you can, but be careful of name contests. Some managers try to find a name by holding a contest among employees. There is no guarantee that such a contest will result in any name that is worthwhile. A second issue is that a contest may obligate you to use a name that will not be effective. Get suggestions but don't promise to use them.

If possible, names or logos should be tested with current and potential customers and any other audience that may be important. When Bell Laboratories became Lucent, the Lucent name was tested with members of the financial community and different types of customers such as network service providers and consumers.

How do you evaluate a name? Here are some criteria:

- Desired associations
- Appealing
- Clear
- Unique
- Memorable
- Easy to spell
- Easy to pronounce
- Sounds good
- Looks good
- Free of potential "new meanings"
- Free of legal threats

Foremost, an effective brand name should have the associations you wish connected to your brand. Die Hard is a very effective name for a Sears automobile battery. The Lucent name was chosen in part because it was associated with "luminous brilliance."

Your brand name should be associated with the attributes that define your brand position.

The name should be unique, easy to remember, sound good, and look good. B. F. Goodrich has suffered from the similarity of their name to that of Goodyear.

As a practical matter, your name must be pronounceable, not only in your country but in any others in which you might do business.

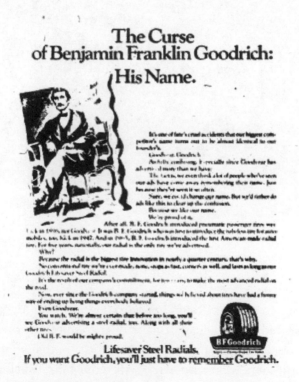

B. F. Goodrich advertisement.

Hoechst, the former chemical giant, ran many ads in the United States seeking to explain how to pronounce Hoechst. Snuggle, the brand name of a fabric softener, is not easy to pronounce in certain languages. While they use different names in different countries, they employ a teddy bear as a constant symbol to cross language barriers.

TRUMP BRAND LOGOS

The Trump brand includes many diverse products and services. However, the type face and presentation of the Trump name remain constant.

Trump Logos
Courtesy of the Trump Organization.

LOGOS

You do not need a graphic design house to develop your logo. The Nike logo was designed by a graduate student at the University of Oregon for a modest amount. However, you do need to be sure that your logo leads to the attributes you want associated with your brand such as the coverage provided by Sherwin-Williams paint or a different kind of coverage provided by Travelers Insurance. Ideally, your logo should be unique. One curious logo example is that of the pink bunny which is used by two separate battery brands throughout the world. Both claim the image and have an agreement as to which countries where they may use it.

CIGNA changed their brand strategy and, consequently, their logo—from block letters to a logo featuring a tree. They wanted to move to a friendlier brand position and did. At the same time that CIGNA changed their logo, they launched a new advertising campaign that was very much focused on people and caring. The CIGNA logo was not changed for the sake of change but because the company brand strategy had changed.

Changing Your Identifier

When you change your identifier, you are changing your brand.

If BMW changes the grill on their automobile, what happens? If Nike changes their famous swoosh, what happens? If Apple changes their apple, what happens?

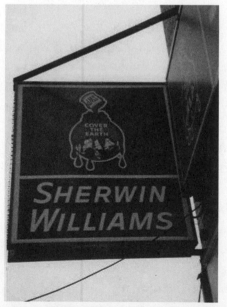

Quick, name an insurance company.

The 35,000 people of Travelers proudly welcome back their classic icon.
Complete with a brand-new stock symbol (TRV) and a new official name: The Travelers Companies, Inc.

TRAVELERS

©2007 The Travelers Companies, Inc. All rights reserved

Sherwin Williams sign and Travelers advertisement.
Photo credit: Don Sexton. Photo courtesy of Don Sexton.

Pink bunny advertisements for Duracell (Germany) and Energizer (Russia)

The first rule about changing an identifier is make sure you need to change it before you do so. Any identifier will have equity. If you discard that identifier, you may be discarding substantial future cash flow. Identifiers should be changed only for compelling reasons.

I was on retainer with a large publishing company and one day received an e-mail from their brand manager. She said that their president was about to change their logo. Why? Because he wanted to—not because of any strategic issues or because of any research findings. For discussion, assume that the logo was a circle and the president wanted to make it a square. Had he done so, the company would have lost their current identity and would have had to spend many dollars to associate an identity with the new logo. Fortunately, we were able to persuade him to reconsider his decision. The logo was refreshed—type fonts were modernized—but it was not replaced.

If strategy requires changing an identifier, it will take time. Sandoz and Ciba-Geigy merged to form Novartis but it took a number of years for the new brand name to be recognized. When considering a new name, it may be quite worthwhile to try to retain some of the existing equity so you are not starting completely anew. For example, when Chase merged with Chemical, they did not walk away from both names. They walked away only from Chemical because Chase had associations they wished to keep—upscale markets and global presence. Be careful of simply adding names together as some accounting firms have done when they merged. Very long names may be difficult to remember and also may be confusing.

Revolutionary/Evolutionary Changes

Revolutionary change is appropriate for those situations when you want a disconnect with the prior identifiers. Such changes occurred when First Union changed to Wachovia, EG&G to PerkinElmer, and ValuJet to AirTran. When Gordon Bethune's team revived Continental, they changed the color and logo to show their new brand position. Revolutionary change can provide a new start.

Evolutionary change preserves existing brand equity. Positive associations of the brand are preserved while keeping it looking fresh and relevant.

Many identifiers seem to have evolved naturally over time. Shell has used the pectin emblem since it was created by Marcus Samuel Jr. in 1900 but it has evolved, becoming more stylized. No change was very radical. Similarly, the Procter and Gamble logo was modernized over time from a rather crude drawing of the moon and stars (with the slogan "this is our soap") to a much more refined rendering.

Logo characters often evolve over time. One famous logo of Pillsbury is the Jolly Green Giant. Initially, the Jolly Green Giant was a scary caveman type who parents might use to scare their children into eating their vegetables. Over the years, Pillsbury got him to work out and get in better shape, straighten up a bit, and dress for success with much better loincloths from a better leaf tailor. Today, he appears as a jovial, friendly fellow with elves playing at his feet. All these changes did not take place in one year but over several years.

The well-known baked goods character, Betty Crocker, has received several makeovers over the years while the Pillsbury Doughboy and the Campbell's Kids have apparently put in some time at the ad character health club and become more buff. The Morton salt girl who debuted in 1914 has changed her frocks over time.

Even if changes are evolutionary, when you change your logo you are changing your brand so it must be done with care. Over the years,

Prudential has used the Rock of Gibraltar as their symbol. It signifies financial stability. The rendering of the Rock of Gibraltar has frequently been modernized. Around 1984 it was modernized to such an extent that, rather than the Rock of Gibraltar, their logo resembled a bar code. They had graphic designed their logo into oblivion. Once they realized what had happened, they quickly returned to a design that could be seen to be the Rock of Gibraltar.

During the 1990s, General Electric changed their logo. Most people did not notice because they made the change carefully. The main change made was to streamline the curlicues on the inside of the logo. Two new logos were under consideration. One was a radically new design, the other the one that was chosen. Had the radical design been selected, everyone would have noticed. The final decision between the two logos was made by Jack Welch. He chose the logo that was an evolutionary not a revolutionary change and that was the correct branding decision. The traditional GE logo represents a significant amount of brand equity. By continuing with that logo, that equity was preserved. In addition, it was not necessary to spend large amounts of money to launch a totally new logo.

Burger King changed their logo to make it more dynamic. They considered several alternatives, including designs with flaming hamburgers. Why flames? Because their brand position includes flame-broiling hamburgers. None of the flaming burgers was the winning design—they appeared a bit fussy and who would want to eat a hamburger that is in flames?

The logo they selected involved only two significant changes in the old logo. They added a third color, blue. The former Burger King logo had just two colors, sort of a reddish color and yellow. Adding blue added punch. The other change was to tilt the burger so that it had more energy. Burger King did not abandon their old look—they changed it to make it more dynamic but it still connects to the former logo. If you were on Mars for five years and came back and saw the new logo, you would still recognize it as Burger King.

Old Burger King logo (Hong Kong) and new Burger King logo (Dublin).
Photo credit: Don Sexton. Photo courtesy of Don Sexton.

Contact Points

Your brand identifiers should be consistently used at every contact point you might have with your customers or potential customers, including:

- Advertising
- Labels
  —On package
  —In use
- Brochures/manuals
- Stationery/business cards
- Signs
- Vehicles
- Uniforms
- Decor

Tyvek advertisement.

Try to be creative in finding new ways to show your name or logo. DuPont's Tyvek brand can be seen across the countryside on the walls of homes being built. Airports have many possible unusual contact points. Citibank has their logo on jetways and Absolut vodka and Singapore Tourism place their name on luggage carousels. The more you can remind your customer of your brand, the more likely they will remember you when they are making a purchase.

CONCLUSION

Brand identifiers are the face of your brand to the world. They need to be chosen to communicate your brand position. Once chosen, they should not be altered significantly unless your brand strategy has altered significantly. Identifiers can be changed over time but care must be taken so that brand equity is not lost due to the changes.

9

Making Sure Your Brands Work Together

Consistency is the key to building strong brands. There are several kinds of consistency—consistency over time, consistency among the brands in an organization, and consistency across markets. Consistency over time concerns how you manage your brand over time and will be explored in Chapter 14, "Keeping Your Brand at Peak Performance."

In this chapter, you learn how to manage brand consistency among all your brands and across all your markets.

Consistency among Your Brands

Together your brands form what is called the *brand architecture*. Consider the three-level brand architecture in Exhibit 9.1. The *master brand* would be like the corporate brand. Its attributes would need to apply to all the brands in the next two levels. The *family brand* would be the brand for a set of products or services, perhaps a division of the organization. The attributes of the family brand would need to apply to all the brands at the *subbrand* level.

For example, the corporate tagline for GE is "Imagination at work." Assuming that imagination is a key attribute of the GE brand, then all the family brands and subbrands under the GE brand should have imagination as one of their main attributes. GE's strategic business units—GE Commercial Finance, GE Healthcare, GE Industrial, GE Infrastructure, and GE Money as well as NBC Universal—should all be known for imagination. Within any of these business units, specific lines of business such as commercial aircraft engines, and specific products such as the GE 90 jet aircraft engine should also be known for imagination.

For a realty company, if the agency is known for its ability to match homes to buyers, then that attribute should be associated with all their

Exhibit 9.1   Levels of Branding*

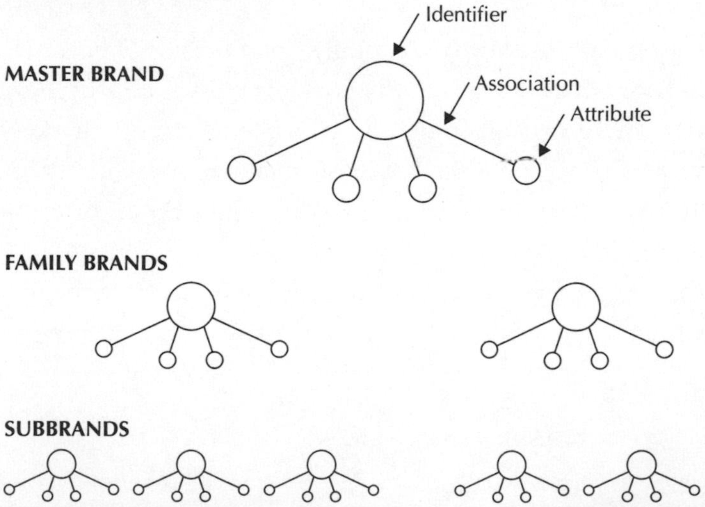

Source: "Arrow Guide—Coordinating Brands," The Arrow Group, Ltd.®, New York, 2008. Used with permission. ***A blank version of this page can be downloaded from www.trumpuniversity .com/branding101 and customized for your personal use.** For any other use, contact Don Sexton at Branding101@thearrowgroup.com.

activities. If an accountant is known for up-to-date tax expertise, than any service he or she performs should be known for that attribute.

If a family brand or a subbrand does not fit into the overall brand architecture, then it may be easier to place it in another brand architecture rather than try to change the attributes of the master brand. For example, the Walt Disney Company is known for wholesome, family entertainment. If they wish to produce a movie with adult themes, they produce it with a different production company such as Touchstone. If they were to try to produce the adult film under the Disney brand, it would both disappoint their customers and cause their brand to erode. Similarly, Levi's once tried to produce men's business suits under the Levi's brand name despite customers telling them that the Levi's brand name stood for products much more casual.

TRUMP ENTERTAINMENT RESORTS ONE CARD

Trump Entertainment Resorts operates three properties in Atlantic City: Trump Taj Mahal Casino Resort, Trump Plaza Hotel and Casino, and Trump Marina Hotel Casino.

Each property has its own brand position but overall they are related by the Trump brand. This relationship is reinforced by the Trump One Card that can be used by guests at any property to enjoy promotions such as cash back on slot play and admission to members-only events.

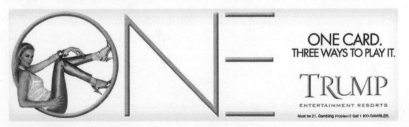

OneCard advertisement.
Photo credit: Michael Spain Smith. Photo courtesy of the Trump Organization.

The Levi's business suits failed but Levi's did produce men's business suits under the name Slate and dress slacks under the name Docker's.

Volkswagen placed VW, Skoda, Bentley, and Bugati in one brand group with an overall position of "class-beating standards" and Audi and Seat in another brand group with the common position of "sportiness, technology, and design." Ford located Aston Martin, Jaguar, Land Rover, and Volvo in their Premier Automotive Group so that their brand images would not be mixed with the brand image of Ford ("Lessons in Successfully Using a Master Brand," *Marketing Week*, May 27, 2004, p. 28).

BUILDING A BRAND ARCHITECTURE

Brand architectures should be built from the ground up. First, the attributes associated with all the subbrands should be considered.

Build your brand architecture from the ground up.

Land Rover produces a number of different models of automobiles including the Defender and the Range Rover. Suppose you were to think of the attributes associated with those automobiles. The Defender is basic transportation but it is considered rugged and adventurous. The Range Rover is luxurious but is also considered rugged and adventurous. The attributes "rugged" and "adventurous" are held in common by all the models in the Land Rover line. Those two attributes would likely be two of the attributes that you would want and expect to be associated with the master brand "Range Rover."

EVALUATING YOUR BRAND ARCHITECTURE

You want your brand architecture to be *coherent*—the brands at all levels working together. If a family brand or subbrand does not fit under the umbrella of attributes of the master brand, then you are not receiving help from the master brand and the brands that do not fit may be harming the master brand.

Steps to evaluate brand architecture:

1. List attributes associated with all your family brands and/or subbrands.
2. Identify attributes associated with the master brand.
3. Compare attributes associated with family brands and/or subbrands and master brand and identify possible gaps or conflicts.
4. Choose attributes to associate with your master brand, family brands, and subbrands.

To evaluate your brand architecture, first consider all your subbrands. Write down the attributes associated with each. Look for attributes that are in common. Subbrands in the same family of products and services should have attributes that are part of the family brand position. If not, then perhaps the subbrand should be repositioned or moved away from the brand architecture. The same is true at the family brand level. The attributes in common across all the family brands should be attributes that are part of the master brand position. If not, perhaps the family brand should be repositioned or moved away from the brand architecture.

Developing Brand Architecture: Family Services Example

Suppose you run a service that provides different kinds of temporary help to families. You have three separate businesses—temporary help for cleaning homes, minding children, or taking care of adults who are incapacitated in some way. You have been using separate brand names for each type of service—"Partners for Cleaning," "Minders for Your Children," and "Helpers for Your Home." You are thinking of using a master brand, Susan's Services, to pull all the subbrands together.

Initially, you might talk to some of the customers or potential customers for each of your three services and ask them what attributes they associate with the service. You also probably have some idea yourself as to what you feel the brand positioning is or should be for each of the three services. For example, suppose "Partners for Cleaning" are known for their reliability in showing up when scheduled and their thoroughness in cleaning. "Minders for Your Children" are known for their creativity in engaging children as well as their punctuality. "Helpers for Your Home" are known for their punctuality as well as their flexibility in dealing with problems.

Given those results, you would likely consider punctuality as one of the attributes that would be associated with the master brand, Susan's Services—"Always there when needed." Before building that brand architecture, you would also want to assure yourself that punctuality is in fact an important benefit to all your customers and potential customers.

The overall brand architecture might look like Exhibit 9.2. Notice that Susan's Services would be known especially for providing help on time. The subbrands would be known especially for their unique benefits such as creativity with children. Whenever one of Susan's Services appears with one of the subbrands, customers would associate punctuality as an additional attribute of that subbrand since it is associated with the master brand. If you wish, you might be able to add another attribute to Susan's Services such as competence.

Exhibit 9.2   Brand Architecture: Family Service Example

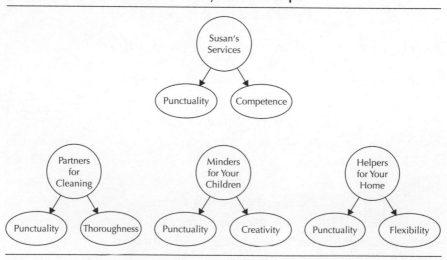

CONSISTENCY OF YOUR BRAND ACROSS MARKETS

Suppose you are selling your product or service in several different market segments. Customers in each market may seek different benefits or have different priorities as regards benefits. Suppose you need a somewhat different brand position in each market but your brand communications will be seen by all the customers in all the market segments. How can you coordinate your branding efforts so that your brand position does not become unclear and confusing to all your target customers?

This problem can occur in domestic markets with multiple segments. Should market segment managers be allowed to develop and implement their own brand strategies? The problem also often occurs with international brands where the markets in different countries require the emphasis of different brand benefits. Should country managers be allowed to develop and implement their own brand strategies? For example, managers of McDonald's in different countries have some leeway in their actions but the overall brand position is similar worldwide.

Should your brand position be the same or different across markets?

If you allow segment managers or country managers to develop and implement their own brand strategies independently, then the brand

McDonald's advertisements (Dublin, Beijing, and Hong Kong).
Photo credit: Don Sexton. Photos courtesy of Don Sexton.

position in each segment will likely be closer to the position desired by the customers in each segment, producing more revenue. However, brand strategies that differ by segment—*if* the customers in the different segments see the different strategies—may confuse customers and make the brand diffuse. Diverse branding efforts will also likely lead to higher branding expenditures as there will be few opportunities to standardize branding activities, such as advertisements, across markets.

COORDINATING YOUR BRAND ACROSS MARKETS

You can find opportunities to standardize your brand across markets by looking *horizontally* across your market segments. The viewpoint of most branding analyses is *vertical*—looking at the customers in a market—and that is very important. However, to coordinate brands across markets, you need to look at what benefits are in common in your most important market segments.

Steps to coordinate brands across markets:

1. List the key benefits for your product or service.
2. Describe the market segments you are considering.
3. For each segment, estimate the priorities for each benefit.
4. Select those market segments that you consider most important.
5. Search for benefits that have high priorities for customers in the those market segments you consider most important.

We successfully followed this approach with one of my clients, a utility company, that was trying to harmonize their brand position across segments they were targeting in the residential market and in the commercial market.

Coordinating Brands across Markets: Truck Example

Suppose you sell heavy-duty trucks in each of three geographical areas. A different manager is responsible for each area and you would like their branding efforts to be coordinated.

Exhibit 9.3   Relative Importance of Benefits by Segments: Truck Example

AREA	A			B			C		
SEGMENT	1	2	3	1	2	3	1	2	3
BENEFIT									
Capacity	9	7	9	8	7	10	9	8	9
Fuel efficiency	9	6	9	8	6	8	10	5	8
Power	6	9	5	8	10	7	7	8	6
Comfort	7	6	10	6	5	9	6	6	10
Ruggedness	5	7	6	6	6	4	6	7	5

Relative importance: 10 = Very important; 1 = Not important.

Segment 1 = Long-distance freight carriers.

Segment 2 = Construction companies.

Segment 3 = Individual contractors.

Source: Donald E. Sexton, "Coordinating Brands Globally," *Global CEO,* July 2007, pp. 9–13. Used with permission. ***A blank version of this page can be downloaded from www .trumpuniversity.com/branding101 and customized for your personal use.*** For any other use, contact Don Sexton at Branding101@thearrowgroup.com.

The first step is to determine the relative importance or priority of the benefits of the product or service for each market segment.

Exhibit 9.3 displays possible benefit priorities for buyers of heavy-duty trucks in each of the three geographical areas. There are three segments under consideration—long-distance freight carriers, construction companies, and individual contractors (owner-operators). Note that this is the Segment Identification Chart discussed in Chapter 6.

Initially, you want to evaluate the segments as to their importance to you—both in terms of their attractiveness (e.g., size, growth rate, price insensitivity) and your relative ability to succeed in the segment. Assume you are not interested in the construction companies—perhaps because you would face strong competitors for their business. That would leave segments 1 and 3—long-distance freight carriers and individual contractors.

To find possible attributes on which to standardize the brand, you need to look *horizontally* across the country-segment chart in Exhibit 9.3.

If you set a relative importance score of 8 or more to reflect high order priorities, then there seem to be two benefits which are highly rated by *both* the long-distance freight carriers and independent contractors in each of the three areas: capacity and fuel efficiency. These two benefits should be considered for inclusion in the overall brand position for both segments of interest in all three areas.

Whether you choose to standardize your brand position on either or both of those benefits depends on your estimate of the impact that standardization would have on your financial performance.

CONCLUSION

Brands rarely work alone. They are related to other brands in your organization in your brand architecture. They are related even if they are being managed in different markets. You must consider those relationships and coordinate your brands. Your brand architecture must be coherent. Your brand communications across markets should be consistent. Without brand coordination, your brands will begin to erode.

10

BUILDING YOUR BRAND FROM THE VERY START

Y ou want to build a brand.

Building a brand requires discipline and patience. It does not necessarily require a lot of money but certainly money helps. Most of all, brand building requires clear market targets, clear brand positioning and clear, consistent brand communications.

In this chapter, you learn the key steps in building a brand.

SUCCESS ROUTES AND FAILURE ROUTES

Which do you build first? Brand awareness? Or value in your customer's mind?

There are a variety of studies that seem to indicate that your first priority in building a brand should be to persuade your customer of the value of your brand to them—the benefits your brand can provide.

For example, Young & Rubicam has developed a rich database, known as the Brand Asset Valuator® or BAV®. The data consists of responses by thousands of respondents in numerous countries regarding their opinions of hundreds of brands. I stress that the following is my interpretation of their findings—*not* Young & Rubicam's interpretation of their findings.

The findings can be summarized in a grid where the vertical axis is related to measures of value to the customer and the horizontal axis is related to measures of brand awareness (see Exhibit 10.1). The data appear to show that you must explain value to the customer first and then connect that value to your brand identifiers. If all branding efforts focus only on building brand awareness, then the customer has no reason to consider your brand. A clear illustration of why brand awareness alone does not work occurred with the numerous dot-com companies that advertised during the 2000 Super Bowl in the United States. Most of those ads were intended to build awareness and they did. Unfortunately, though, most of them provided no reasons for the customers to purchase the products or services and the following year many of those companies were out of business.

Exhibit 10.1   Brand Dynamics

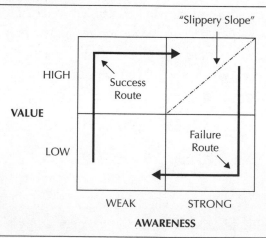

Adapted from Brand Asset Valuator®, Young & Rubicam, yr.com, 2008.

You must explain value to your customers first, then link value to your identifiers.

Brand awareness alone does not build a strong brand. Customers must know your brand name *and* what it stands for in terms of benefits. Shortly before TWA went out of business, the TWA brand had high awareness according to the BAV® study. What those customers were saying was, "I know you but I don't like you."

How to Build a Brand

To build a brand, you need to develop a brand strategy as discussed in Chapter 6. Because you are creating a new brand, the canvas is empty so your first major choices are determining your target market and brand positioning. Because your target customers may not know you, you will need to place more emphasis on the content and timing of your brand communications.

Steps in building a new brand:

1. Understand your customers.
2. Evaluate your product or service.
3. Select your target market.
4. Determine your desired brand position.
5. Design and implement your communications strategy.

TRUMP HOTEL COLLECTION

The Trump Hotel Collection includes properties in New York City, Chicago, Las Vegas, Dubai, Waikiki, Toronto, Panama City, and many other locations. Donald Trump described their positioning: "Each hotel will be distinguished by outstanding architecture

---

(continued)

Trump Hotel Collection advertisement

created by some of the finest architects in the world and complemented by the highest level of personalized service."

Many of the developments combine residential units with hotel accommodations. All rooms are spacious with luxurious furnishings by firms such as Bellino, Stearns and Foster, Subzero, and Miele. The properties include world-class dining as well as pampering at The Spa at Trump, with exclusive Kate Somerville skin-care products and a selection of treatments designed for each location.

Jim Petrus, chief operating officer of Trump International Hotels Management LLC, observed, "The preeminence of the Trump name in the real estate market makes us uniquely qualified to succeed in the luxury hotel arena and bring it to a global market. As a new brand, Trump Hotel Collection offers a unique opportunity for the Trump family to make its mark on the international luxury hospitality market."

Architecture is used to distinguish the properties. Each hotel has its own distinctive—often bold—design.

Source: "Introducing Trump Hotel Collection," The Trump Organization press release, October 10, 2007.

Understanding Your Customers

As always, branding begins with thoroughly understanding your customers—why and how they purchase and what benefits they are seeking. Suppose you are an entrepreneur starting a company to provide wedding advice. You need to talk with some potential customers and find out what they want and what they like or do not like about existing wedding planners. If you are beginning a vending machine network, you need to talk with some potential customers and find out what they want and what they like or do not like about existing vending machine services. Whatever the business for which you are building a brand, your brand strategy must begin with your potential customers.

Evaluating Your Product or Service

What does your product or service do well? Does it provide a benefit that your potential customers want? Do you have a competitive advantage that will allow you to sustain that benefit advantage?

If you do not find a competitive advantage, you should probably not try to sell that specific product or service to customers in that particular market. A product or service with no competitive advantage (and therefore no benefit advantage) is known as a *commodity*. Commodities are sold only on price as there is no basis for differentiation on benefits and consequently it may be difficult to build a brand position. Unless your organization has the lowest costs (or is in a protected market), it is very difficult to succeed with a commodity.

Targeting Your Market and Determining Your Brand Position

As discussed in Chapter 6, your target market are those potential customers on which you will focus your brand efforts. You choose them based on your relative ability to win them and on the attractiveness of the market with respect to revenue, profits, or cash flow and then develop a brand position you believe they will find appealing.

When Bell Laboratories started building the Lucent brand, they found that associations with Bell Labs included positive attributes such as reliability and technology but also some negative attributes such as inflexibility and arrogance. As a result, they designed their brand programs to keep the old positive attributes, lose the old negative attributes, and add new positive attributes such as "can do" and user-friendly (Peter L. Phillips and Stephen A. Greyser, "Creating a Corporate Identity for a $20 Billion Start-Up," Boston: Design Management Institute Press, January 1, 1999).

Communicating Your Brand Position

Generally it is much easier to build your brand earlier than later. The longer you wait, the more likely you are to encounter competitors with similar brand positions and the more likely you are to find customers who are no longer excited by the product or service category.

THE PIONEER

The key for a pioneer—the first entrant in a product or service category to build a brand—is to develop the product category. But at some point the pioneer must also—at the same time—make the argument as to why their brand is superior. Otherwise a fast follower can enter the market and take over the market for the product category that the pioneer has developed with much effort and expenditure.

If you are the first one in a market—perhaps an entrepreneur with a new idea for a product or service—then you are the pioneer. You will find that customers will usually not know you and that the competing products and services will be those products or services that your target customer is already using to solve their problem—often based on old technology.

Lack of customer knowledge of your new business means that you must place special emphasis on *communicating* your brand position to your target customers. Not only must the target customers know what you do and why they should buy from you, they must also think of you when they have a need which your product or service can satisfy. In short, start-up brand strategies typically must deal with what we called in Chapter 3 the "left-hand side" problem—building the association between the customer and the brand of your product or service—what

iPod advertisements.

is known as the *ability to launch*. iPod was initially positioned for their impressive design, then moved to the joy of using an iPod.

Ability to launch is the ability to educate customers. That requires understanding of how target customers receive their information and what information sources may have the most impact on their behavior. For example, potential customers for software may rely on what they find on the Internet while potential customers for a new type of health club may rely on what their friends say. A software entrepreneur should plan brand communications for the web while the proprietor of the new type of health club should try to generate word-of-mouth.

The contents of the communications should link the customer's problem to your solution as described in your brand position. If the brand position of the health club were focused on rapid weight loss, then the brand message might consist of: "Need to look good this Friday—come to us on Monday for safe, quick weight loss." If the brand position were based on getting in shape, the message might be: "Want to feel energetic—come to us for proven programs for getting in shape."

Remember that customers who do not know what your product or service does may not be appreciative of what you can do for them. They often have inertia. You must connect their problem to your—better—solution.

If you need to use resellers, the same may be true of them. They may be skeptical of your new product or service. Therefore you will have to show them how effective your argument is in persuading your target customers to try your product or service. Mattel launched Barbie in the Czech Republic with a major event in the leading department store in Prague.

The pioneer's entry strategy may be what is known as a *skimming strategy* or *a penetration strategy* or some mix of the two.

A skimming strategy is tightly focused on specific market segments—usually customers who might be expected to be first or early adopters of the new product or service. For example, digital cameras were first offered to journalists and military personnel. The advantages of a skimming strategy include fewer resources required—especially cash—and

Introduction of Barbie in Prague department store.
Photo credit: Don Sexton. Photo courtesy of Don Sexton.

acquisition of customers who may be more willing to try the product or service and possibly pay premium prices for it.

Skimming strategies are appropriate when there are relatively few customers and the market is growing slowly. That allows the pioneer time to develop their brand without incurring major expenditures.

In order to skim, the entrepreneur needs to have understanding of which customers may be most appreciative of their product or service. There needs to be enough of them to build a profitable business early on. For example, if you have developed a modular deck for suburban homes, you must be able to identify those homeowners interested and willing to purchase such a deck and they must be sufficiently numerous to provide you with acceptable sales and profits.

The major drawback to a skimming strategy is that you have shown your product or service and your brand position so others might be able to imitate you. If possible, you need to have some type of *entry barrier* that will prevent competitors from copying and succeeding with a product or service similar to yours. Entry barriers include patents or copyrights but may also be based on specific knowledge or experience. A restaurant may offer a special cuisine because they have one of the few chefs who can create those dishes.

In the long-run, there are no entry barriers. The entrepreneur must be prepared for the eventual entry of competitors but better competitors enter later than sooner.

In the long run, there are no entry barriers so build your brand sooner than later.

The opposite strategy to a skimming strategy is the penetration strategy. With a penetration strategy, you try to saturate the market and build your brand position before your competitors do. Usually penetration strategies are employed with large markets where no entry barriers are possible and speed-to-market is essential.

Penetration strategies generally require substantial financial resources for both operations and for marketing, particularly communications. The advantage of a penetration strategy is a potentially high long-term return if the product or service is successful and the creation of an *installed base*—customers who may be expected to be loyal over time. The disadvantage, of course, is the relatively high short-term cost associated with a penetration strategy.

Penetration strategies should be considered when there appear to be numerous target customers—who might be expected to have high *switching costs*. A switching cost is the cost a customer incurs if they switch suppliers. For example, if a customer is using a graphics program and has all his or her files stored in the format for that program, there is a conversion cost—perhaps large—to convert all those files to be compatible with a new graphics program. Your brand can also be a switching cost to your customer—the trust you build up may persuade him or her to continue purchasing from you rather than try an unknown brand. The switching costs preserve and protect the installed base and, in a way, are like having entry barriers around individual customers.

Brand penetration strategies are most effective where there are *experience curve effects* on cost. Experience curve effects are decreases in costs due to learning, due to various economies of scale, and due to the spreading out of fixed costs over a larger unit volume. A reseller of computer components would likely receive larger discounts the more units they purchase and the expenses of their headquarter operations would be spread over more volume the more stores they have.

Skimming and penetration strategies are two extremes. You can also follow a *modified skimming* strategy. With such a strategy, you begin by skimming—by focusing on specific target markets—then gradually pursue more and more market segments, perhaps eventually targeting much of the market.

The Fast-Follower

Fast-followers have products or services similar to that of the pioneer but enter the market just a bit later. At that time, the market is usually beginning to grow rapidly. Customers at this time are usually much more knowledgeable. That means they are more capable of differentiating among competing brands of a product or service. More knowledgeable customers make it possible for the fast-follower to enter successfully during this stage—providing they can persuade the customers of the superiority of their brand. (See the sidebar on Maxim versus Taster's Choice.)

Incidentally, the warning for Pioneers is to continue to improve their own product or service so as not to leave an opening for the fast-followers. If pioneers do not evolve their product, the chances for the fast-follower to succeed increase.

Fast-followers must have competitive intelligence and understand what their competitors offer their target customers and how they might be planning to improve. Fast-followers must find a brand position superior to those of their competitors—either because they have superior performance on a benefit or because they provide new benefits of importance to their customers. That may require the ability to reverse-engineer the competitors' products or services—find out what they do well and how they do it. Fast-follower entrepreneurs may also require the skills of lawyers who can determine what they can apply from what their competitors have done.

Fast-followers can achieve a stronger brand position by developing a product or service superior to their competitors' products or services in the views of the current target customers. They can also achieve a stronger brand position by targeting customers different from those currently served by their competitors. If a new type of health club has opened and is focused primarily on individuals in their 30s and 40s, then you might open a similar health club aimed at individuals in their 50s and 60s or in their 20s.

Fast-followers, of course, need to be *fast*. The longer they wait to enter a market, the more likely it is that the pioneer will build a strong customer base.

Just as with the pioneer, the brand-building strategy of the fast-follower can vary in scope. The strategy can be focused on one or two key segments—much like a skimming strategy. Or the strategy can be focused on several segments—similar to a penetration strategy. Small resources and a product or service with highly selective appeal would favor the tightly focused strategy. Large resources and a large potential market would favor the multiple segment strategy.

As regards brand communications, the time when the pioneer and fast-followers meet is perhaps the most crucial time for building a brand position. During this stage, the customers are very knowledgeable and able to distinguish among brands. This is the time to communicate very clearly your brand position and why it is superior to the positions of your competitors' brands.

**When the pioneer and the fast-followers meet
is perhaps the most crucial time for building
a brand position.**

SIDEBAR: MAXIM VERSUS TASTER'S CHOICE

In the late 1960s, a company today known as Kraft researched the U.S. market for coffee. They found that the only coffees available were brewed coffees—perceived to be rich-tasting but messy to prepare—and instant coffees—perceived to be watery-tasting but easy to prepare (Exhibit 10.2). What people said they really wanted was a rich-tasting, easy-to-prepare coffee.

Kraft used processes from the U.S. space program and introduced a freeze-dried coffee, Maxim, that was richer tasting than the current instant coffees and was also easy to prepare. Maxim quickly achieved a 10 percent share of the instant coffee market.

Meanwhile, Nestle was developing their own freeze-dried coffee. They introduced it with the tagline, "You know what

Exhibit 10.2   Perceptual Map: Coffee

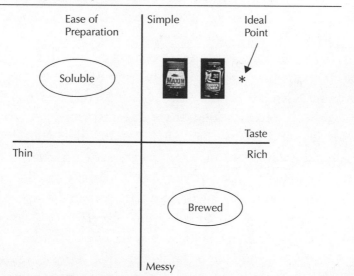

Source: "Arrow Guide—Formulating the Brand Strategy," The Arrow Group, Ltd.®, New York, 2008. Used with permission.

(continued)

freeze-dried coffee is, now taste the best, Taster's Choice."
Within two years, Taster's Choice overtook Maxim and Maxim
never regained their lead. Over those two years, Taster's Choice
charged the same price and spent less money on advertising!
When Kraft finally removed Maxim from the market in the late
1990s, Taster's Choice had a market share more than 30 times
larger than that of Maxim. The power of a well-chosen and well-
communicated brand position!

Source: Peter Flatow, "Beyond 'Me Too'-ism: Being Second Isn't All Bad," *Adweek,*
September 22, 1986.

The Slow-Follower

Sometimes you are entering a market that is already crowded. To build
your brand successfully in such circumstances, you either need a brand
position that is exciting and unmatched by any existing competitor or
you need a huge amount of cash.

Slow-followers face intense competition—either from many imitators competing on price or from a few well-entrenched competitors
or both. Nonetheless, if you are entering a market late, it is possible to
succeed. However, the odds may be against you. If you are opening the
tenth dry cleaner in a small neighborhood, then your dry cleaner will
need to be unique in some way that is very attractive to the potential
customers. Perhaps your dry cleaner has a special technique for removing stains without damaging fabric. If so, then that special benefit will
be a key part of your brand position. Or perhaps you will remain open
24 hours—again that would be your brand position.

Without distinction on some benefit of interest to the target customers, you will likely need to out-spend your opponents—with advertising, promotion, and whatever else you can think of. Generally, it
may be wiser to try to find a benefit advantage for your brand that is
superior to those of your competitors' brands.

MANAGING YOUR BRAND

Once you build your brand, you need to manage it. Chapters 11 though 14 focus on different kinds of brand management situations such as rejuvenating a brand and extending a brand. You can see the relationship among all these situations with the growth matrix (Exhibit 10.3).

The growth matrix is usually credited to Igor Ansoff, a pioneer in strategic planning. Usually it is employed to generate growth opportunities and to spotlight risk. The two axes of the matrix represent the two dimensions in which an organization might grow—the product or service direction and the market or customer direction. Product or service opportunities are described as current, related, and new. Current products and services are ones the company provides at present while related or new products or services are ones it might provide. For example, a wedding planner might consider a related service of offering advice for parties of all sorts or a new service of beginning a school for wedding planners.

Exhibit 10.3   Growth Matrix

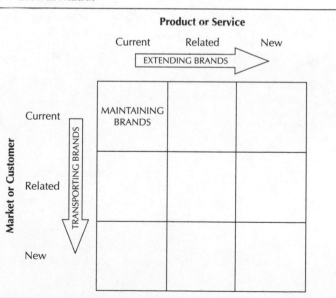

Source: "Arrow Guide—Managing the Brand," The Arrow Group, Ltd.®, New York, 2007. Used with permission.

Market or customer opportunities are also described as current, related, and new. A wedding planner who has focused his or her efforts on couples in their 20s and 30s might consider a related market of couples in their 40s and 50s or a new market in another geographic area.

Branding situations in the upper left corner of the growth matrix—current customers and current products or services—concern maintaining your brand, for example, rejuvenating your brand or handling a brand crisis. Branding situations along the top row of the matrix concern extending the brand. Branding situations along the left column of the matrix concern transporting the brand, including developing a global brand.

All these situations are explored in the following chapters.

CONCLUSION

Successful brand building is a lot easier with a product or service that is highly differentiated from the competitors—on a benefit that customers care about. Generally that means that it is much easier to build a brand earlier than later. Once your brand is built, your responsibilities have just begun. Now you face decisions about how to keep your brand strong and prosperous—the focus of the following chapters.

11

NEW LIVES FOR OLD
BRANDS

If you have a brand that was once strong but is now tired and weak, you have a terrific opportunity. Brands retain their value for a long time. With appropriate attention and effort, an old brand can be rejuvenated—often in a relatively short time period. The managers of exhausted brands often have great opportunities to achieve quick brand turnarounds.

HARLEY-DAVIDSON: REVIVING A LEGEND

At one time, Harley-Davidson held nearly 100 percent of the U.S. motorcycle market. By 1981, the Japanese companies had secured 94 percent of the U.S. motorcycle market. How did this happen?

(continued)

Harley allowed the Japanese motorcycle companies into the United States by not blocking their entry with small motorcycles. Honda, Yamaha, Kawasaki, and Suzuki entered the U.S. market with small bikes and then gradually moved into the larger sizes. At that time, the Japanese manufacturers were much more efficient producers than Harley, spent more on advertising than Harley, and produced bikes which were more reliable than Harley's.

During this time, American Machine and Foundry (AMF) merged with Harley-Davidson. They tripled production and quality control declined. The joke was that "You needed two Harleys in order to have spare parts to keep one on the road." A proud brand was being hollowed out.

In the 1980s, Harley-Davidson made a recovery that many still consider miraculous—employing innovation and branding.

Harley-Davidson managed their costs down. They cut their workforce by 40 percent and decreased salaries by 9 percent and froze them for two years. They visited the factories of their Japanese competitors, learned techniques such as just-in-time inventory, and made cost-saving innovations to their production lines. They also began programs to increase quality control.

Meanwhile, their chief designer, William "Willie G." Davidson, bought them time through innovation, by designing new Harley models such as the Super Glide that did not require substantial retooling. These new designs allowed Harley to increase their perceived value in the short run while waiting for their longer-term efforts to pay off.

Many of these changes would not have been possible except that thirteen Harley managers succeeded in purchasing the company away from AMF in 1981. Harley-Davidson did receive trade protection but in fact it was not very effective. Of more significance was the Harley buff who approved the loan that kept Harley afloat during the tough times—another illustration of how strong branding can help.

WOULD YOU SELL
AN UNRELIABLE MOTORCYCLE
TO THESE GUYS?

Harley-Davidson motorcycle advertisements.

Even though Harley refurbished their motorcycles, the associations of value needed to be reestablished in the customers' minds. *After* they had fixed their product problems, Harley ran several ads to inform their customers and potential customers. One memorable print ad showed a group of tough-looking motorcyclists with the headline, "Would you sell an unreliable motorcycle to these guys?"

The combination of process and product innovation and branding worked. By the end of the 1980s, Harley-Davidson had a 30 percent share of the overall U.S. motorcycle market, including nearly two-thirds of the large (over 750 cc) motorcycles. Today, the brand remains powerful, with considerable loyalty among their riders who say, as the ad does, "I believe the machine I sit on can tell the world exactly where I stand."

Source: Peter C. Reid, *Well-Made in America,* New York: McGraw-Hill, 1991; and Richard A. Melcher, "Tune-Up Time for Harley," *BusinessWeek,* April 8, 1996, pp. 90–91.

How to Fix a Tired Brand

Here are five steps for fixing a tired brand:

1. Perform a brand diagnosis to determine the weakness.
2. Understand how the brand became tired.
3. Clarify your target market and brand positioning.
4. If necessary, modify your product or service.
5. Reformulate your branding tactics, especially your branding communications.

The French Foreign Legion rejuvenated their brand in 2001. They were no longer obtaining sufficient recruits from Europe so they increased their efforts in other markets, especially Latin America and Asia, and employed web sites to communicate to potential recruits the Legion's promise, "A new opportunity for a new life." The result: Their Latin American and Asian recruits increased by more than 50 percent—not bad for an organization with a slogan "March or Die."

Brand Diagnosis

Chapter 22 discusses different measures that you might employ in a scorecard to monitor your brand. Some of the recommended measures are shown in Exhibit 11.1.

- *Name recall* is the percentage of customers who know your brand name.
- *Differentiated* is the percentage of those who recall your brand name who think your brand is different from other brands.
- *Relevance* is the percentage of those who think your brand is different who think it is different in a way that is important to them.
- *Brand trial* is the percentage of those who think your brand difference is important to them who try your product or service.

Exhibit 11.1 Brand Diagnosis

Brand	Name Recall (%)	Differentiated (%)	Relevant (%)	Brand Trial (%)	Customer Satisfaction (%)	Recommend (%)
A	80	60	60	50	40	40
B	80	60	60	50	10	5
C	80	60	15	15	10	10
D	80	20	15	15	10	10
E	20	60	60	50	40	40

Source: "Arrow Guide—Diagnosing the Brand," The Arrow Group, Ltd.®, New York, 2008. Used with permission.

- *Customer satisfaction* is the percentage of those who try your brand who are satisfied with it.
- *Recommend* is the percentage of those who are satisfied with your brand who recommend it to others.

Were you to see percentages such as those in Exhibit 11.1, you might interpret them as follows:

Brand A is generally healthy—relatively high percentages for all the measures. People know the brand, think it's different in ways they care about, try it, are satisfied with it, and tell others.

Brand B likely has a problem with the product or the service. People are persuaded to try the product or service but find they don't like it when they use it. For this brand to be rejuvenated, you first must fix the product or service.

Brand C likely has a problem of relevance. People consider the brand different but not in any way that they care about. To rejuvenate this brand you may have to reposition it or find a new target segment or both.

Brand D seems to have a problem of differentiation—high recall but relatively few people know how it might differ from other brands. This problem might be due to the brand positioning or to a failure in communications to make clear how the brand differs from other brands.

Brand E probably has a problem related to the amount of branding effort expended. Those who know about the brand consider it relevant, try it, like it, and tell others about it. The problem is that too few people know about the brand. This problem might be solved with a higher level of communications expenditure.

Notice that cases B, C, and D all show high brand awareness even while the brands are in trouble. Brand awareness by itself is not a useful measure of brand strength.

Why Brands Get Tired: Hollowing Out

When an organization cuts back on the resources given a brand—either for operations including quality control, product or service improvements, or communications, then the brand may be "hollowed out"—the Brand B scenario in Exhibit 11.1. Often the motivation of hollowing out a brand is to improve financial returns. Brands are valuable because they lead to retained customers—customers who believe the brand promise. Even if the brand promise is no longer being kept due to a hollowing out strategy, customers may persist in buying the brand. When they eventually realize that the brand has changed, then they will abandon it. The hollowing out of a brand is the beginning of the failure route discussed in Chapter 10 (Exhibit 10.1) and nearly happened to Harley-Davidson (see Sidebar).

Why Brands Get Tired: Off-Target Brand Strategy

Strong brands are built with clear strategies and consistent tactics. Wrong market targets or wrong positioning can make a brand irrelevant—the Brand C scenario. Mountain Dew had been positioned for suburban youth. Beginning in the late 1980s, a seven-year branding campaign repositioned the brand to be edgier and more relevant to all 15- to 18-year-olds.

Constant changes in brand communications can lead to a brand with no focus—the Brand D situation, high name awareness but little understanding as to what the brand stands for. For nearly 30 years, Burger King changed their advertising almost yearly. Why? In part because they kept changing managers and advertising agencies. Similarly, for many years MasterCard ads seemed always to be changing until the "Priceless" campaign stabilized their brand.

Why Brands Get Tired: Overextending

Too many brand extensions can blur the brand position and also create Brand D conditions. Brand extensions can dilute the brand position of the master brand. At one point, Pierre Cardin licensed hundreds of products—more than any other brand in the world. The consequence was the brand was no longer clear in the mind of many customers. Similarly, in the 1990s, the YSL and Gucci brands were placed on numerous products, causing brand dilution. In all these cases, the numbers of licenses were reduced so that the brands could regain their strength (John Carreyrou and Alessandra Galloni, "Can Gucci Make Its Other Labels Profitable?" *Wall Street Journal*, November 6, 2003, p. B-1; and John Carreyrou and Cecilie Rohwedder, "Style & Substance: In Again at Gucci," *Wall Street Journal*, March 5, 2004, p. A-9).

When Helmut Panke, CEO of BMW, was asked how they keep the BMW brand consistent, he replied, "The biggest task is to be able to say, 'No' . . . when something doesn't fit, you must make sure that that is not done" (Neal E. Boudette, "BMW's CEO Just Says 'No' to Protect Brand," *Wall Street Journal*, November 26, 2003, p. B-1).

Why Brands Get Tired: Inattention

A brand can become tired simply through inattention—leading to any of the Brand B, C, and D scenarios. *Penthouse* magazine, once a powerhouse, languished for many years due to a lack of attention. A dynamic manager has revived the magazine with new graphics, new articles, new formats, and is focusing the market clearly on males in their 20s. The new brand position is for the magazine to be like a club, with advice tailored to the needs of the 20-something male, whether it be clothing, automobiles, or relationships.

CLARIFY TARGET MARKET AND POSITIONING

Key to the rejuvenation of Mountain Dew was the reformulation of its brand strategy. Research showed that Mountain Dew had been perceived as a suburban or even rural brand. Pepsi targeted the brand toward urban teenagers. Mountain Dew had been known for sports. That attribute was kept in the brand positioning but it was moved to extreme sports. The attitude of Mountain Dew was made edgier and irreverent. The repositioning process took about seven years but moved Mountain Dew into the number three position among their target market.

MODIFY PRODUCT OR SERVICE

Rejuvenating a brand may not require only changing communications—you may need to rejuvenate your brand by improving the product or service. Customers will continue to purchase a strong brand for a while despite any product or service problems. However, once customers realize your product or service no longer performs as it once did, they will leave.

You must keep your brand promise or your customers will leave.

148

In 1982, British Airways (BA) was losing money and their advertising agency, Saatchi & Saatchi, conducted a survey of airline passengers in the United Kingdom, United States, France, Germany, and Hong Kong. (By chance, I was one of those surveyed.) BA was seen to be a large experienced airline using modern equipment, but received low ratings on friendliness, in-flight service, punctuality, and value. They initiated a major overhaul of their customer service operations. For example, they empowered their customer service representatives to solve customer problems such as lost luggage immediately rather than over a period of weeks. The result—after several years of a very successful communications campaign—was to elevate BA to the position of second most profitable airline in the world (Paula Dwyer, "Air Raid," *BusinessWeek*, August 24, 1992; and John A. Quelch, "British Airways," HBS, 1984).

Steinway's faced product difficulties when they had a change of ownership and consequent change of management in the early 1990s. Their brand was extraordinarily strong but the production process changed so that dealers and customers began to complain about the sound of the piano; customers even paid a premium for pianos built *before* the new management had taken over. Steinway's was turned around when a musical instrument company, Selmer, purchased them and restored their production values to their legendary levels ("Piano-Making at Steinway," *New York Times*, March 28, 1991; and "Sour Notes," *Wall Street Journal*, March 27, 1991).

REFORMULATE BRANDING TACTICS

Even though you have changed your brand strategy—targets and positioning—you must still persuade the customer. You will likely need to develop new brand communications to tell your new story.

Miller Brewing needed to develop communications to retarget and reposition Miller Lite but did not find that easy.

The initial ad campaign for Miller Lite featured retired athletes from baseball, football, and other sports as well as author Mickey Spillane.

The ads were famously entertaining but apparently resulted in the demographics of Miller Lite drinkers skewing toward older men.

Miller Brewing tried to attract younger drinkers with a variety of campaigns but none seemed effective. An ad agency, Fallon McElligott, developed a campaign that was—tongue-in-cheek—created by a "creative super star" named "Dick." In the words of the first ad, "each ad has a beginning and an ending, but in between, anything can happen." This campaign was targeted toward the legal drinking age to 25-year-old market.

Miller Lite advertisement.

Old Spice advertisements over time.

The campaign was undeniably a change in their communications. However, it may not have been on-strategy. The "anything can happen" segments of the ads often were outrageous and it was not clear to everyone what they had to do with "Miller Time" or with Miller Lite. Initially sales increased 2.5 percent but the campaign was discontinued after about two and a half years (Enrico Dottie, "Miller Campaign Falls Flat with Viewers," *USA Today*, March 10, 1997, p. 6B).

Two and a half years is not usually sufficient time to determine if a campaign is working. However, changing communications does not rejuvenate a brand unless it builds the brand position with customers in the target market.

Old Spice was long regarded as "your grandfather's aftershave." Procter & Gamble successfully changed that position with an aggressive communications campaign. With each ad, they raised the intensity of the Old Spice experience. One ad even poked fun at their old image with the line, "If your grandfather hadn't worn it, you wouldn't be here."

CONCLUSION

A tired brand is an opportunity—an opportunity to build a strong brand on an already existing foundation. First, you need to discover what caused the brand to become tired. You may need to change the target markets and positioning and improve the performance of the product or service. You will certainly need to change the brand communications. Above all, you must be consistent as you build your new brand position. The rewards can be immense.

12

GROWING YOUR BUSINESS
BY EXTENDING YOUR BRAND

Bic perfume? Bausch & Lomb mouthwash? Clairol's Touch of Yoghurt shampoo? Levi's men's business suits? Pond's toothpaste? Jack Daniel's beer? All were failed brand extensions (Mark Ritson, "Don't Catch Brand Extension Disease," *Marketing*, August 29, 2007, p. 21).

When you have a strong brand, you can use it as a platform for growth by extending it to other products or services. Target customers will already know what your brand stands for and that will possibly lead to high perceived value even before you introduce the product or service. However, you need to think through brand extensions carefully. Your brand may not extend to the new category. And if it does extend to the category, the extension may have a negative impact on the master brand.

In this chapter, you learn how to generate and evaluate brand extensions that make sense and that will be profitable for you.

BRAND EXTENSIONS

Brand extensions are one means for growing your business—using your carefully built brand equity to move into new product or service areas. To extend a brand, you need to discover the current attributes associated with the brand, then use them to move your brand to a new category of product or service. If there is no attribute that takes you to that new category, then it will be difficult to make that brand extension.

Brands are extended through current associations.

For example, Hershey is associated with the attribute "chocolate." That means it is relatively easy to extend the Hershey brand to other products that involve chocolate such as milk, topping, cookies, or ice cream (see Exhibit 12.1). It would not be impossible to extend the Hershey brand to other products such as strawberry topping but it would be more difficult and more expensive to do so. Smucker's is associated with strawberry jam so could likely extend to strawberry topping but would find it more difficult than Hershey to extend to chocolate topping. Old Spice is associated with men's aftershave and can move easily to deodorant while Nivea cream can follow the bridge of moisturizing from women to men.

Cosmopolitan magazine has aggressively extended their brand and their brand extensions in clothing, lingerie, hosiery, eyewear, swimwear, accessories, and watches retail in more than 4,000 outlets in Europe (although they failed with Cosmo yoghurt; James Bainbridge and Esther Lake, "Brand Extensions," *Media Week*, September 6, 2001; and Alex Benady, "Love the Mag? Now You Can Taste It Too," *Evening Standard* [London], December 12, 2001, p. 46). Virgin has used their values of irreverence, fun, and challenge to extend their brand into a great many areas—more than 200 corporate entities—although not all these ventures have been successful (Mark Ritson, "Virgin's Brand Power Obscures Its Lack of Success in Extension," *Marketing*, August 1, 2002; and "Path to Extension," *Marketing*, October 20, 2004, p. 35).

Exhibit 12.1   Brand Extension

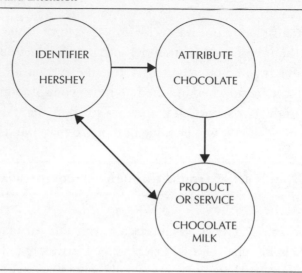

Source: "Arrow Guide—Extending the Brand," The Arrow Group, Ltd.®, New York, 2008. Used with permission.

In the United Kingdom, Jane Packer has used her brand association with flowers to extend her three tulip trademark to shops, schools of floral design, vases, fragrances, candles, bed linen, greeting cards, and garden equipment ("Jane Packer, Florist, Grows the Brand," *Brand Strategy*, June 6, 2001, p. 13). In South Africa, Kulula used its brand position as a low-cost airline to develop an online travel site for booking hotels, holiday packages, and automobiles (Adele Shevel, "Unlikely Brand Extensions a Risk Worth Taking," *Sunday Times* [South Africa], January 20, 2008, p. 7).

Many failures to extend brands occur because there is no obvious attribute to bridge the gap between the brand and the new category (see Exhibit 12.2). Rubber Maid could not extend to computer work stations since the attributes associated with their brand are low-tech. Brown-Forman failed to extend the Jack Daniels brand to charcoal briquettes—Jack Daniels is filtered through charcoal but that is not an effective bridge for an extension. Harley-Davidson was unsuccessful extending their brand to cigarettes but was very successful extending their brand to motorcycle gear such as jackets and boots—where there is a natural bridge. Oil of Olay had difficulty expanding to cosmetics, according to Peter Shaw, a marketing consultant, "because the mother brand has an intimacy about it that cannot be transferred to a cosmetics range, which is all about being overt and looking good from the outside" ("Power Brands Begin to Stretch Credibility," *Marketing Week*, December 12, 2002, p. 19).

Exhibit 12.2   Unsuccessful Brand Extensions

Master Brand	Extension
Levi's	Men's business suits
Rubbermaid	Computer work tables
Jack Daniel's	Beer
Jack Daniel's	Charcoal briquettes
Bausch & Lomb	Mouthwash
Stetson	Umbrellas
Mr. Coffee	Coffee

Source: "Arrow Guide—Managing the Brand," The Arrow Group, Ltd.®, New York, 2008. Used with permission.

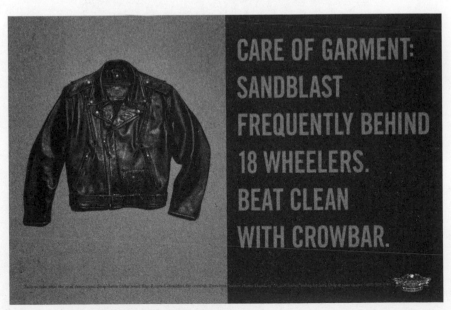

Harley-Davidson motorcycle gear advertisement.

TRUMP HOME® RUGS

Trump Home® rugs are produced in a partnership between The Trump Organization and Miresco Decorative Rugs. Amir Mireskandari, president and CEO of Miresco Decorative Rugs, noted that "Trump Home® is one of the most highly sought after brands [by retailers]."

The carpets are hand woven from New Zealand wool and are organized in two collections, Westchester™ and Central Park™. The Westchester™ designs consist of rich colors and patterns that reflect the sophisticated lifestyle of Donald J. Trump, while the Central Park™ designs are influenced by modern, metropolitan concepts with a bit of Art Deco.

Trump Home® Rugs.
Photo courtesy of the Trump Organization.

> In keeping with the position of the Trump brand, the rugs are designed to have upscale appeal, yet be affordable to members of their target market. They provide a logical extension to the Trump Home® product line that also includes furniture, lighting, and fine art, allowing customers "to create a coordinated, elegant and sophisticated look for their homes at an affordable luxury price point."
>
> ―――――――――
>
> *Source:* "Trump Home Floor Fashion Debuts at Atlanta International Rug Market," The Trump Organization press release, June 26, 2007.

STEPS TO EXTEND A BRAND

You can be systematic about brand extension decisions by following these four steps:

1. Examine attributes currently associated with brand.
2. Evaluate possible brand extension opportunities.
3. Consider possible consequences of brand extensions and their likelihoods.
4. Select brand extension opportunity.

Examine Attributes Currently Associated with Brand

The starting point for determining a brand extension is to inventory all the attributes that target customers likely associate with the brand. How do you find this out? By asking the target customers what they think of when they consider the brand identifier (name, logo, color, etc.).

McDonald's and Burger King brands have associations with children. For example, McDonald's has often had alliances and promotions with the Walt Disney Company. Both McDonald's and Burger King have frequently given away toys. A strong brand association with kids is great when you are marketing to children but *not* if you want to market to adults.

McDonald's launched a sandwich—the Arch Deluxe—which was supposed to be targeted for adults to help McDonald's expand from reliance on children as customers (Bruce Horovitz, "Arch de Triumph?" *USA Today*, June 14, 1996, p. 1 B). The Arch Deluxe was a major failure for many reasons but one of the reasons was that the McDonald's brand would not support a sandwich for adults at that time. In the United States, the fast-food hamburger company that is associated with adults is Wendy's. When my friends at Wendy's heard about the launch of the Arch Deluxe, their attitude to McDonald's was, "Bring it on—make my day" because Wendy's managers know that in the United States their brand has owned the adult fast-food hamburger market.

Note that strong or dominant brands typically cannot be easily extended. As you will recall from Chapter 3, dominant brands own an attribute such as a category. Goodyear is a dominant brand for tires and expended much effort to extend their brand to automobile repair in Canada. Levi's is a dominant brand for jeans and was not able to extend the Levi's brand to men's dress slacks.

Strong or dominant brands are not easily extended.

Weak brands are also difficult to extend. Because there are no attributes strongly associated with weak brands, there are no attributes to be the bridge to the new product or service category to which the brand is to be extended.

Brand extensions are most likely to be successful for brands that have neither very weak nor very strong associations.

Evaluate Possible Brand Extension Opportunities

Each of the attributes associated with the brand in turn will suggest brand extension possibilities. For example, if one of the attributes of a brand of soap was its moisturizing effect, then possible extension opportunities would include moisturizing creams and lotions.

As discussed in Chapter 6, there are two major dimensions to evaluate market opportunities: Attractiveness and Relative Ability. Attractiveness depends on the characteristics of the opportunity such as size and growth of market. Relative ability concerns how likely you are to succeed with the opportunity and is based on your capabilities to win the target market. The Segment Selection Chart (Chapter 6) can be applied to sort out the extension opportunities.

Consider Possible Consequences of Brand Extensions

Whenever you are considering a brand extension, you always want to look at associations in both directions. You need to look at the strength of the association between your brand and the new product or service category. But you also must consider any associations from the new category back to your brand. Evaluate associations not only outgoing but incoming.

Sometimes a brand extension can actually hurt you rather than help you. There are many examples. Suppose I say Bausch and Lomb, what do you think of? Probably contact lenses or eye care. Bausch and Lomb tried to extend their brand to mouthwash. Most people when they hear this example say, "eeeew." Just as a quick test, if people say "eeeew" when they hear a possible brand extension it is probably not going to be successful. You don't even have to do the marketing research. Just keep that in mind so when you are sitting around with all the C-level executives and the CEO says "eeeew"—don't do the extension.

Bausch & Lomb did try the extension and it failed. All they had to do was move two inches on the face from the eyes to the mouth but they could not do it. But notice if they had been successful, most likely the association with mouthwash would have had a negative impact on their eye care business.

You need to look both directions whenever you are looking at the associations involved with a brand extension.

Select Brand Extension Opportunity

Finally, you select your brand extension opportunity based on your evaluation of the attractiveness of each opportunity, your relative ability to win, and your estimate of the likely effects of any consequences due to each brand extension.

As Cathy Hoffman Glosser, executive vice president of global licensing for The Trump Organization, cautions, "Our key objective, with all of [our licensing] deals, is to find the right partners and not expand so quickly that we can't give our partners the support they deserve. We want to choose partners who fit in well with the mix we've already started to put together" (Julie Naughton, "Building Trumpland," *WWD*, December 16, 2004, p. 1).

Clothing Example Suppose you have a small business called "Laura's Winter Clothing." Friends and acquaintances knit sweaters that you then sell on the Internet or to local retailers. You are thinking of extending your brand to other products.

An inventory of the attributes associated with your brand would certainly include "sweaters," but suppose they might also include "winter," "clothing," "warmth," and "warm colors" (see Exhibit 12.3).

Exhibit 12.3   Attributes and Opportunities Audit*

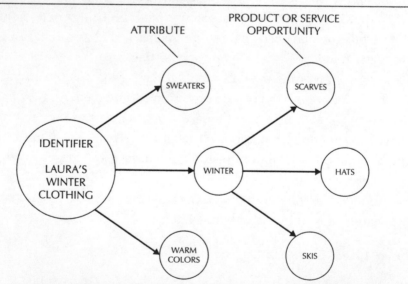

Source: "Arrow Guide—Extending the Brand," The Arrow Group, Ltd.®, New York, 2008. Used with permission. ***A blank version of this page can be downloaded from www.trumpuniversity.com/branding101 and customized for your personal use.*** For any other use, contact Don Sexton at Branding101@thearrowgroup.com.

How does Laura know this? She has talked with and e-mailed her customers to find out what they associate with her brand.

She considers each of the attributes and where they might lead. For example, "winter" might lead to products people use in the winter such as scarves, hats, skis, parkas, and gloves (see Exhibit 12.3). "Warm colors" might lead to other kinds of clothing such as blouses, shirts, and slacks.

Each of these possible opportunities is attractive in that they each might represent a large market. Most likely what she will do will depend on her relative ability. Her organization has high capability to produce knit goods (and no capability at all to produce skis) so scarves, hats, and gloves would seem to be a good fit for her.

Adding scarves, hats, and gloves to her line would likely not have any negative impact on her current brand and, in fact, may enhance it as it would reinforce the "winterness" of the brand. Scarves, hats, and gloves would seem to be promising brand extensions.

Notice how the name of her organization both enables and constrains her growth options via brand extensions. "Winter" leads directly to a lot of items but not items used in the summer and "clothing" would not be associated with items such as skis. Had she named her organization, "Laura's Sweaters," her growth options would be more limited. However, had she named her organization, "Laura's," her growth options would be much less limited *but* she may have had more difficulty in getting her business started because "Laura's" would be unspecific and it would be more difficult to build her brand initially.

Whether to use a very specific brand name or a very general brand name is always an issue for a start-up.

BRAND EXTENSION OPTIONS

Brand extensions can be direct. In a direct extension, the brand name is applied to a new product or service. With direct extensions, the brand is at maximum risk. If for some reason the new product or service does not succeed or if the attributes associated with the new product or service are somehow inconsistent with the original brand, then the brand can be damaged.

Indirect brand extensions do not rely as much on the brand as do direct brand extensions. Consequently, the brand is at some risk but not at maximum risk. There are various kinds of indirect brand extensions such as hidden brands and temporary brands.

Indirect brand extensions lower the risk of extensions to the master brand.

Hidden brands are used when you do not want the attributes associated with your master brand or family brand to be associated with a particular subbrand. With a hidden brand, no indication is given in the brand communications that the subbrand is related to the master brand. For example, Saturn automobiles are produced by General Motors but the General Motors brand is not featured in advertisements for Saturn. Marriott owns the Ritz-Carlton chain of hotels but does not use the Marriott name in connection with the Ritz-Carlton name. Red Dog beer was brewed by SAB Miller but Miller was not usually mentioned in their ads. Bartles & Jaymes wine coolers were produced by Gallo.

Hidden brands insulate the subbrand from the attributes of the master brand. There is a risk with some hidden brands that, if customers were unaware of the association with the master brand, they may be surprised when and if they find out and possibly react negatively.

Temporary brands are used when the subbrand can benefit from an association with the master brand but will not bear the main responsibility for the performance of the product or service. For example, when Black & Decker purchased the small appliance operations of GE, they were allowed to utilize the GE brand name for a short time afterward while they transitioned the brand to Black & Decker. Similarly, the IBM name was used on Lexmark printers while they developed their own Lexmark brand position.

Temporary brands can also be used to introduce customers to a new brand. Marriott describes their Fairfield Inn chain of hotels as

"Fairfield Inn by Marriott." The Marriott brand in effect is introducing Fairfield Inn to the customer but the Marriott brand would not be seen as taking full responsibility for the experience of a Fairfield Inn. The Fairfield Inn experience would be the responsibility of the Fairfield Inn brand.

Co-brands can increase the long-term return on an organization's brand investment. A co-brand has the potential to provide a net increase in revenue and profits through higher demand and price for the co-branded product or service—*if* the partner brands have a positive synergy. As in any alliance, risk may be shared among the partners, making the venture more attractive.

Co-brands combine the attributes of two or more brands. The co-brand attributes are a mixture of the attributes of those of the partner brands. An effective co-brand occurs when the attributes of the two brands complement each other. For example, many credit cards involve a bank and either Visa or MasterCard. The banks provide their particular brand attributes that may include financial expertise while the credit card organization provides brand attributes such as wide acceptability.

Co-brands combine the attributes of two or more brands.

In the case of Tata-BP Lubricants India, BPAmoco provided the lubricant experience while Tata contributed local trust and automotive knowledge. Betty Crocker combines their baking experience with taste from Hershey's to form a co-brand for brownies. The World Wide Fund for Nature collaborated with Christy's, a leading manufacturer of towels in the United Kingdom, to create a co-brand perceived as both environmentally friendly and attractive (Tom Blackett and Bob Boad, eds., *Co-Branding*, London: Macmillan, 1999).

Curves is a well-known brand name of a network of workout centers specifically for women. The brand's associated attributes include weight loss. General Mills is a well-regarded and well-known producer of breakfast cereals. They cooperate to co-brand a whole-grain cereal that is low-calorie—utilizing the associations of both partner brands ("Survey Reveals Best, Worst Brand Extensions," *Progressive Grocer*, January 8, 2008).

The rules of co-branding also apply to ingredient branding (e.g., NutraSweet, Teflon) and celebrity endorsements. On occasions when a celebrity endorser becomes embroiled in some well-publicized difficulties, the co-brand partner often drops the celebrity from the campaign. Some years ago, there seemed to be renewed interest in employing as endorsers celebrities no longer living such as James Dean and John Wayne—possibly because there was less chance for embarrassing behaviors to be discovered.

Curves Cereal from General Mills.

From the point of view of branding, the key concern of co-branding should always be what will be the impact of the partner's brand—positive or negative?

OVEREXTENDING A BRAND

The Kit Kat brand from Nestle Rowntree has been extended in many ways—some observers feel at times in too many ways. A few years ago, Richard Murray, director of the Williams Murray Hamm brand consultancy, stated, "Lots of marketing people think it is easier to do brand extensions than to do something really new. This can have an insidious long-term effect. Kit Kat is a great iconic brand that is being pulled to pieces" (Andy Hoffman, "More Kit Kats Is Good. Too Many Is Not," *Globe and Mail* [Canada], September 9, 2006, p. B 3; "When Extension Can Become Overstretch," *Marketing Week*, August 19, 2004, p. 23; and "To Stretch or Not To Stretch," *Grocer*, April 22, 2006, p. 40).

Kodak's first corporate brand manager, a friend of mine, told me one of his first actions was to review and cut back on the number of products licensed to use the Kodak name. Many of those licensing agreements seemed to have been arranged for short-term financial gains with little thought to their impact on the value of the Kodak name. The licensed products included chalk—white chalk—not likely to help the Kodak brand.

GROWTH OPPORTUNITIES

You can examine all your growth opportunities by using the growth matrix (Exhibit 10.3) and the brand extension matrix (see Exhibit 12.4).

The growth matrix was discussed in Chapter 10. It is used to generate growth opportunities and to spotlight risk. The two axes of the matrix represent the two dimensions in which an organization might grow—the product or service direction and the market or customer direction. The more you move away from your current products and services and your current markets and customers, the more risk you take on. That is because the more you depart from what you are

Exhibit 12.4   Growth Opportunities

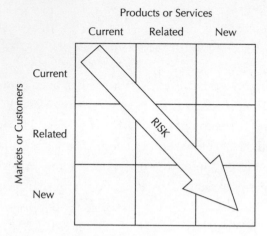

Growth Matrix

Brand Extension Matrix

Source: "Arrow Guide—Extending the Brand," The Arrow Group, Ltd.®, New York, 2008. Used with permission.

currently doing, the more knowledge you need to acquire regarding products or services or markets or customers.

The growth matrix spotlights important concerns for making selections among growth opportunities by relating growth moves to an organization's capabilities. However, the growth matrix does not capture the risks due to brand extensions. From the point of view of the growth matrix, it made perfect sense for Levi's to produce men's business suits. Levi's has the cutting and sewing capabilities to be successful making men's business suits. Levi's men's business suits failed—not because of their operations capabilities but because of their brand's ability to stretch to the new product category.

When considering brand growth opportunities, you need to consider both the growth matrix and the brand extension matrix. I developed the brand extension matrix to capture the risks associated with brand extensions.

When extending a brand, you need to consider not only what your organization can do but also what your customers will let you do.

The brand extension matrix has the same dimensions as the growth matrix, namely, products or services and markets or customers. However, the brand extension matrix spotlights risk due to extending a brand. The further you move from your current brand position regarding products or services and markets or customers, the higher the risk you face. From the viewpoint of the brand extension matrix, the venture of Levi's to make men's business suits was very risky.

Selecting growth opportunities requires you to *overlay* the growth matrix with the brand extension matrix. The growth matrix tells you what your organization *can* do. The brand extension matrix tells you what customers will *allow* you to do.

CONCLUSION

Brands can be a platform for growth. However, brand extensions involve risk, both to the product or service to which you want to extend the brand and to the master brand itself. Brand extensions must not be thought of as simply licensing opportunities. They need to be evaluated in the broader context of the brand strategy and the organization's strategy.

13

WHEN THINGS GO WRONG

Tylenol, Union Carbide, Andersen, Coca-Cola, Audi, Ford, Firestone, Perrier, Diet Pepsi, Intel, Bon Vivant, Jack-in-the-Box, and numerous politicians—these are just some of the brands that have gone through crises due to real or supposed problems with the product or service. Some weathered the branding storm, others foundered.

Hopefully your brand will never have a crisis. However, if it does, you may want to look over this chapter. Here you learn how to survive a brand crisis.

WHAT IS A CRISIS?

A crisis is not the same as a problem. Crises have the potential to *harm* your reputation and your organization. Perrier lost more than a quarter of their U.S. market share of bottled water as a result of a crisis involving alleged traces of benzene and they never fully recovered

(Norman Klein and Stephen A. Greyser, "The Perrier Recall," Harvard Business School, 1990).

A crisis is any situation that may:

- Cause harm.
- Escalate in intensity.
- Fall under scrutiny.
- Interfere with your operations.
- Damage the organization.

A crisis often has harmed customers or has the potential to do so. According to one manager of a crisis center service, "A client's first thought is always to protect the image of the brand and the first call it tends to make is to the PR agency. But, while that is important, so too is getting the product off sale, communicating to customers quickly and protecting the space at retail, which is vital to the health of the brand" (Robert Gray, "Coping with a Crisis," *Marketing*, July 3, 2003, p. 25).

Managers feel extreme pressure during crises because they want to prevent further harm. Typically crises escalate—more and more people become affected. Justifiably, crises are covered by the news media and receive the attention of the public and politicians. Crises interfere with your operations and have the potential to destroy your brand and put you out of business.

Managers who have experienced a brand crisis tell me it is like a fire storm. It often happens suddenly and is stunning. The crisis is seen as a threat but it is not clear how serious it might be. The effects of the crisis pervade the organization and managers feel they must take action but may not be sure as to what they should be doing.

A brand crisis is like a fire storm.

During a crisis, the normal rules and procedures of the organization are disrupted. It is difficult to understand what is happening—what is happening seems incomprehensible. There is a lot of information —often an information overload—but uncertainty increases. The choices available seem limited and irreversible.

The impact of a crisis on managers is to cause anxiety, stress, fatigue, and, consequently, possible mistakes in decision making.

How to Handle a Crisis: Diet Pepsi

In Seattle, Washington, June 10, 1993, there were reports of a syringe found in a can of Diet Pepsi. On June 13, a similar claim occurred in New Orleans. By June 14, Pepsi had assembled their crisis team, including their president-CEO of North America, Craig Weatherup. On June 15, Pepsi provided newscasts with video of their production line, showing how Diet Pepsi cans were inverted immediately before they were filled so that there was no possibility that a hypodermic needle could be placed in the can before it was sealed. As shown in Exhibit 13.1, release of the video broke the back of the crisis—the number of news items dropped rapidly.

Exhibit 13.1   Diet Pepsi News Reports

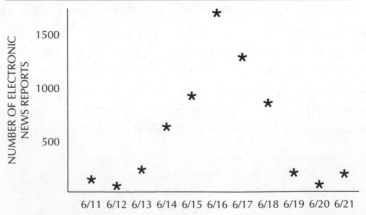

Source: PepsiCo records, 1993.

WHEN THINGS GO WRONG

Dr. David Kessler, Food and Drug Administration Commissioner, also appeared on television. He initially assured the public that there was no evidence that any of the needles had been contaminated. Subsequently, he stated that it was unlikely that there was any nationwide scheme to tamper with Diet Pepsi. According to Dr. Kessler, "Reports of possible tampering breed additional reports; it is a vicious cycle. That is what we believe has happened here."

By June 17, several people had been arrested and charged with filing false reports that they had found syringes in their Diet Pepsi cans, including one woman caught by a surveillance camera placing a syringe into an opened can. Throughout, Weatherup communicated Pepsi's concern over the reports and detailed what Pepsi was doing. No cans were recalled and estimates indicated that the crisis had little impact on the sales of Diet Pepsi. Pepsi's handling of the crisis was textbook correct.

Source: Marcy Magiera, "Pepsi Weathers Tampering Hoaxes," *Advertising Age,* June 21, 1993, pp. 1, 46.

Much of the research concerning how managers perform during crises shows behavior similar to that when families face tragedies such as illness or death. Behavior differs as to whether the crisis was unanticipated or anticipated and whether preparations were made beforehand to deal with the crisis.

If the crisis was not anticipated and not prepared for, then the initial attitudes are denial and disbelief. During the crisis, panic may set in and, after the crisis, radical changes may be made. In contrast, if the crisis was anticipated and preparations taken, managers feel more in control—even during the firestorm.

Reaction to unanticipated crises is often denial and disbelief.

MANAGING A CRISIS

If a crisis occurs, you must take charge immediately. You have to get by the denial feelings as quickly as possible and realize that something has happened and you need to deal with it.

Remember that as time moves along, the chances of the crisis to cause harm and, if so, to cause substantial harm increase while the number of alternatives to manage the crisis become smaller. The quicker you take hold of the crisis situation, the more likely you will obtain a satisfactory resolution to the situation.

It took Coca-Cola's CEO several days to fly to Brussels to respond to reports of illness among Belgian children allegedly due to Coca-Cola products. Intel initially kept quiet regarding flaws in their Pentium processor ("Crisis, What Crisis?" *Brand Strategy*, August 21, 2002, p. 20).

During the crisis involving Firestone tires and Ford Explorers, Bridgestone, the owner of Firestone, waited three months after the start of a government investigation into possible accidents before they began a tire recall program—which was to be *phased* in gradually. As a consequence, Moody's reduced their credit rating from A2 to negative based on the likely impact of their slow actions on future sales (Fiona Walsh, "Botched Recall Puts Skids Under Bridgestone," *Evening Standard*, August 16, 2000, p. 37; and George Vernadakis, "Where Marketers Fear to Tread: Firestone's Wheel of Misfortune," *Advertising Age*, August 21, 2000, p. 29).

It is crucial that you obtain information on the crisis—as much as you can and as quickly as possible. You need to find the cause of the problem so you can fix it. When in doubt, assume the worst. When someone placed cyanide in the Tylenol packages in Chicago some years ago, Johnson & Johnson immediately cleared the shelves of all product.

During a crisis, it may be difficult to absorb information and determine what is important. Therefore, you should invite the opinions of others who are not so immersed in the situation and can give you an arm's-length view of what seems to be going on.

One approach to understanding the crisis is to construct scenarios as to what might have happened and what will happen. For example, in the Tylenol crisis, one scenario was that it was an isolated incident. A scarier scenario was that many packages in many cities had been tampered with. Johnson & Johnson chose to take no chances and assumed the worst case.

Given your scenarios, you develop your crisis strategy. That may involve disposing of product or otherwise changing your operations. However, you must fix the problem as soon as possible. When there were reports that one model of a Mini gave off a warm vapor and a popping noise whenever it was filled with gasoline, Mini management found the source of the problem—flammable paint on the fuel tank pipe in some cars—and fixed it immediately. The BMW corporate communications manager in the United Kingdom observed, "You fix [the problem]—you don't try to just pull through" (James Hall, "What to Do If Your Brand Becomes a Turkey," *Sunday Telegraph*, February 11, 2007, City, p. 7).

An especially important part of your strategy consists of your communications—who will speak for your organization, to whom will they speak, what will they say. Communication should be honest and calm. You need to emphasize first that you are concerned. Then you must explain that you are in charge, are finding out what has happened, and are taking care of the problem. More communication is much better than less.

In March 1987, 188 people died in the Herald of Free Enterprise ship tragedy. Their CEO declared on television that their procedures would not let a vessel leave port with the bow doors open while live video from a helicopter showed the ship on its side with open bow doors—not a stance that would build credibility ("Crisis, What Crisis?" *Brand Strategy*, August 21, 2002, p. 20). In contrast, when an Alaska Airlines flight crashed in January 2000, killing 88 people, Alaska Airlines made their web site into a site for crash information which was updated hourly (Dana James, "When Your Company Goes Code Blue," *Marketing News*, November 6, 2000, pp. 1, 15–16).

PREPARING FOR A CRISIS

Unfortunately, you need to assume a crisis will affect your brand. If you prepare for the crisis, you will be able to handle it more effectively and there will be less harm to people and less damage to your organization.

To prepare for a crisis, there are four steps you should follow:

1. Make clear that crisis response is an organization priority.
2. Organize a crisis team and have a crisis center prepared.
3. Set up information systems.
4. Develop stand-by plans for a crisis, including crisis communication strategy.

The first step in crisis preparation is to acknowledge that a crisis might occur. That requires scenario thinking. You should assemble a group of your employees and ask the question, "What could happen to cause a crisis?" Possible causes should be identified such as product problems, natural disasters, employee behavior, or outsider actions.

The crisis team should include:

• Senior management
• Market or product experts
• Operations experts
• Other experts
• Legal experts
• Outsiders
• A spokesperson

The core crisis team for Diet Pepsi consisted of the president and CEO, the vice president of public affairs, and the vice president for scientific and regulatory affairs. They were supported by specialists such as legal counsel and directors of consumer relations and development and procurement. Outsiders included various media and public relations experts.

All team members should be capable of working under stress and be able to focus immediately on the crisis situation and what may need to be done.

At least one senior manager should be on the team to provide it with authority both internally and externally. Depending on the nature of the crisis, you may need access to expertise—product, market, operations, or perhaps some other area. Of course, your team will need legal advice.

Outsiders should be on the team to provide you with perspective. When you are inside the fire storm of a crisis, often it is difficult to gain objectivity as to what is happening and how it is being perceived.

Outsiders should be on the team to provide perspective.

The spokesperson might be any member of the team. However, it would be most helpful if the senior manager might take that role as that will give more clout to what the crisis team wishes to communicate. The spokesperson must have media skills. That is, he or she needs to be comfortable with the press and able to clearly state the situation, describe the concerns of the organization, and what is being done to fix the problem.

Information must flow freely to the crisis team. There must be early warning sensors to inform management if, for example, there seem to be problems with a product. Bad news must travel easily through the organization—in some organizations, bad news is deleted or does not travel easily. Before the Coca-Cola crisis in Belgium, observers alleged that Coca-Cola averaged 40 complaints per month and then suddenly received 25,600 complaints in 11 days—if so, that should have been a signal that something was amiss ("Crisis, What Crisis?" *Brand Strategy*, August 21, 2002, p. 20).

A stand-by plan should be prepared for each possible crisis scenario. When an actual crisis occurs, it is often very difficult to put together a plan due to the intensity of the situation. A stand-by plan can always be changed but it provides a starting point. The stand-by plan should include the communications plan—key audiences such as police and fire departments, media, the public, the government, and employees—and how and what will be communicated to them. Generally, the more transparent the organization's response, the more effective the handling of the crisis.

Communicating internally and externally is the key to managing a brand crisis.

The crisis plan should be tested by having the team go through crisis simulations where they can experience their roles and practice their responses.

AFTERWARD

Once the crisis is over, keep in mind that you need to continue to communicate to your customers and others that the situation is again normal and, perhaps, improved.

CONCLUSION

Brands can be destroyed by crises if they are not managed. Of much more importance, people can be harmed if a crisis is not dealt with quickly. Throughout, communications with the public should be maintained. For crises to be managed, they must be anticipated. Plans need to be ready in case a crisis occurs. Consider it good fortune if the plans never need to be used.

14

KEEPING YOUR BRAND
AT PEAK PERFORMANCE
OVER TIME

Should you change your brand strategy over time?

Your brand strategy will likely need to change due to changes in customers and competitors. However, keep in mind that you will want to keep your brand position as consistent as possible.

This chapter is your tour of the stages of the competitive life cycle. You examine the competitive conditions for each stage and you learn what kind of branding strategy you need to win during each stage.

TYPES OF LIFE CYCLES

Competitive conditions in an industry change every moment. Customers become more knowledgeable. Competitors become more aggressive. New technology emerges. All these changes may lead you to change your branding approach.

> **You need to watch your competitive environment so you will know when changing competitive conditions require you to change your branding strategy.**

Life cycles describe how competitive conditions change. A life cycle charts how unit sales may be expected to change over time.

There are three major types of life cycles (see Exhibit 14.1):

1.   Market life cycle
2.   Product or service life cycle
3.   Model life cycle

The market life cycle consists of the demand by customers to satisfy a need or solve a particular problem. For example, a need might be the need to communicate with others at a distance or to have a quick meal. Note that the word *problem* is used in the marketing sense—a customer need to be satisfied. Generally, market life cycles increase with the number of customers who have the particular need.

Exhibit 14.1   Types of Life Cycles

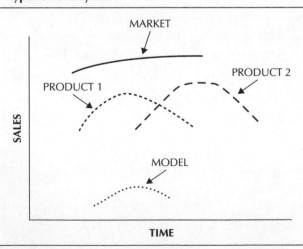

Source: "Arrow Guide—Managing through the Competitive Life Cycle," The Arrow Group, Ltd.®, New York, 2008. Used with permission.

The product or service life cycle refers to a specific way to satisfy a customer's need and shows how unit sales change over time. Often the product or service is related to a technology. For example, the need to communicate at a distance has and can be satisfied with smoke signals, drums, radio, telephone, cellular telephones, and e-mail. Meals can be purchased from full-service restaurants, diners, street vendors, and fast-food restaurants. Product life cycles typically have stages when growth climbs, plateaus, and then falls—due to the emergence of new products or services. Consequently, product life cycles tend to be much more volatile than market life cycles.

Product life cycles come in many shapes and sizes. We are not using the product life cycle as a predictive model but as a *descriptive* model. There are statistical methods for predicting sales over time, such as regression analysis and exponential smoothing, but that is not our focus here.

Product life cycles come in many shapes and sizes.

The model life cycle concerns specific versions of a product or service. Illustrations would be different models of a particular cellular telephone or different types of heavy-duty trucks or different types of apartments in a condominium or different types of catered parties. For some categories, the model life cycle can be very important. For example, in industries involved with fashion or entertainment, styles can change very quickly and that affects the model life cycles.

THE COMPETITIVE LIFE CYCLE

The product life cycle describes how competitive conditions change over time in a specific product or service category and that is why a more accurate name is the *competitive life cycle* (see Exhibit 14.2).

During the Introduction stage, there is one organization—the pioneer—providing a new product or service. The competition is all those organizations still providing the old way of doing something—the

Exhibit 14.2   Product or Service Life Cycle

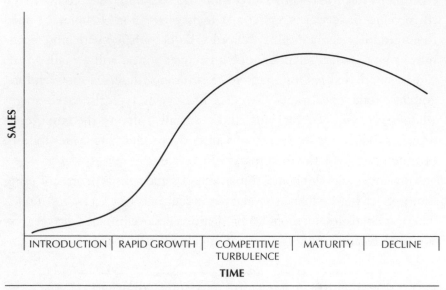

Source: "Arrow Guide—Managing through the Competitive Life Cycle," The Arrow Group, Ltd.®, New York, 2008. Used with permission.

old technology. For most products and services, growth is slow during the Introduction stage—that allows entrepreneurs to begin their businesses.

In the Rapid Growth stage, sales begin to take off. There are usually a handful of direct competitors in the market. They include the pioneer and what are known as the *fast followers*—organizations that enter right after the pioneer.

The Competitive Turbulence stage is usually characterized by price competition. Why? Because now many other organizations (the *slow followers*) are entering with products or services that imitate the ones already on the market and often they have excess capacity. Similar products and excess capacity and slowing market growth is a recipe for a price war—especially if you have not yet built your brand. Only a few organizations will survive this stage, which is why it is also known as the "shake-out." Market segments emerge in this stage so you must be sure to focus your marketing efforts to members of your target market segments.

The Maturity stage may be very long or very short, depending on the pace of technological change in the industry. Growth now is related to population or industrial sector growth and competitors are often consolidating. Customers are usually very knowledgeable and their purchases are often routine. Suppliers and resellers are often partners. During this stage, it is often very difficult to differentiate your product or service among customers any more than you have already done.

The Decline stage occurs because a new product or service has appeared which satisfies customer needs more effectively than the current product or service. Consequently sales decrease and end-users and resellers are no longer interested in the product or service. Eventually the demand for the current product or service will disappear or be considerably diminished. If you wish to continue to sell to your customers, your brand must embrace the new technology—the new product or service—that is displacing the old technology.

Most marketing textbooks do not distinguish between Rapid Growth and Competitive Turbulence. On a slow day, I went through the numerous marketing textbooks I have in my university office and I found that 80 percent of them, including several best-selling texts, combined the Rapid Growth and Competitive Turbulence stages into one stage that the authors typically called Growth. Much of the utility of the competitive life cycle rests on the distinctions among the stages. Unfortunately, in 80 percent of marketing texts some of that utility has been removed.

Margin, Cost, and Perceived Value Curves

The competitive life cycle shows how your sales may change over time. However, there are three other curves that help explain how your competitive conditions may change over time (see Exhibit 14.3).

Suppose you define unit margin as price less unit cost. Typically, the unit margin curve begins negative in the Introduction stage, becomes positive and often reaches its maximum during the Rapid Growth stage, plunges during Competitive Turbulence due to price competition, stabilizes for a while during Maturity, and then falls again during the Decline stage.

Exhibit 14.3   Competitive Life Cycle

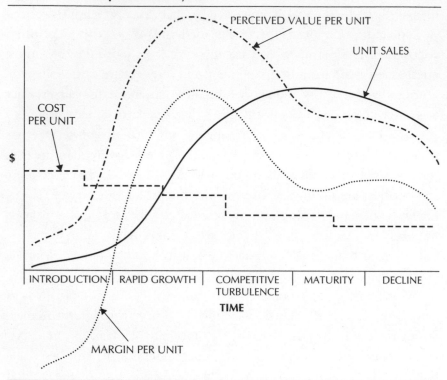

Source: "Arrow Guide—Managing through the Competitive Life Cycle," The Arrow Group, Ltd.®, New York, 2008. Used with permission.

The unit cost curve often starts high due to prototype costs and the costs of the initial sell-in. Then, unit cost falls as managers succeed in managing their operations. Note that decreases in unit costs are not an automatic effect, but reflect diligent cost-cutting efforts. Firms unsuccessful at cost-cutting are shaken out.

The final curve is crucial—the perceived value curve. Recall from Chapter 4 that perceived value is the maximum the customer is willing to pay for your product or service. Perceived value is not price; it is the ceiling on price.

During the Introduction stage, the perceived value curve begins low, then increases during the Rapid Growth stage. Frequently, perceived value peaks in the Rapid Growth stage before the me-too competitors enter. The decline in perceived value (which is always relative to competing products or services) that occurs during Competitive Turbulence may be halted during the Mature stage. However, when a new competing technology appears, perceived value falls again throughout the Decline stage.

The shapes of the margin curve and other curves described below may vary due to special circumstances. However, in numerous executive seminars I have conducted, managers confirm that the curves drawn in Exhibit 14.3 are consistent with what they often see as they manage their products and services.

You need not stay throughout the entire competitive life cycle, but, if you do, here are brand strategies to consider.

INTRODUCTION STAGE

During the introduction stage, your branding strategy must explain to your target customers the value of the new technology versus the old technology. This is basic marketing and basic branding—yet nearly all the biggest disasters in the history of marketing (Polavision, RCA Video Disc, Premier cigarettes) are characterized by not talking to customers about their needs and then not educating them about how the new product would meet those needs better than existing products or services.

In contrast, one of the very first manufacturers of video games, Atari, used their initial ads to address concerns with video games such as whether they would harm a television set, then used later ads to describe why their brand was best. In one of their early ads, FedEx convincingly demonstrated why their shipping service was superior to the existing service, air freight forwarders.

Brand strategies include *Penetration* and *Skimming*. Penetration consists of trying to take over as much of your target market as possible before someone else enters. If you are running a health club and it is the first in an area, a penetration strategy might include an initial membership promotion to try to sign up as many members as possible before another health club opens its doors.

Source: Company records

Early Federal Express advertisement.

Skimming requires you to focus on certain customers, ignoring the others. For example, you might start your health club by focusing only on high-income members willing and able to pay high fees for special attention from expert personal trainers. In the long run, you may start with a skimming strategy, but then broaden your focus to other customers as Armani and Ralph Lauren have done with their lines of clothing.

In the year 2000, many pioneering dot-com companies spent huge amounts of money on advertising, yet most of them failed because they were not able or did not try to educate customers and build value in their minds. For example, Pets.com was an Internet service where people could order food and other supplies for their pets. Pets.com raised over $130 million and spent much of it on television ads on the United States professional football championship game—The Super Bowl.

As a result, they created high brand awareness and persuaded many people to visit their site—but relatively few made a purchase and their losses in the last quarter of 1999 and the first two quarters of 2000 totaled $125 million on sales of less than $23 million. Their share price began at $11 and fell to $1.38 in just six months. When they went bankrupt, probably their most valuable asset was a dog sock-puppet—the spokesperson in their ads.

Pets.com was never able to convince sufficient target customers that buying pet supplies from them was attractive. Their tag line was "because pets can't drive." While it was true that pets can't drive, unfortunately for pets.com the pets' owners were able to drive to the supermarket or pet store (Debra Aho Williamson, "A Dog's Life," *Advertising Age*, August 7, 2000, p. S10; and Patricia Riedman, "Sock Puppet Joins Homeless," *Advertising Age*, November 14, 2000, p. 86).

RAPID GROWTH STAGE

The main characteristic of this stage is that now you have direct competitors. These are the fast followers who have entered the market soon after your launch. At the same time, your customers are starting to become very knowledgeable—and demanding—regarding their expectations.

If you are a pioneer, the key skill you need in this stage is the ability to continue to improve your product or service in evolutionary ways so you can maintain the differentiation of your brand. Besides design skills, you need competitor information capability so that you know what will be the key benefits of your competitors. However, you especially need to be able to manage a dual-focus brand communications strategy. A dual-focus communications strategy means that some of your communications remain focused on educating the customers and developing the market and that other communications are focused on building your brand by spotlighting your brand position. For example, you might explain why health clubs are important to gain new customers and at the same time explain why your health club is superior (a wider variety of equipment, longer hours, etc.) to current health club members.

During the Rapid Growth stage it is essential that you put distance between your own product or service and those of the competitors.

Now is when it is most likely you will have a major functional—or, better, emotional—benefit that is superior to that of your competitors. Now is the time to associate that benefit with your brand—you want to *own* that benefit. DuPont is often a pioneer and has often successfully defended their position as with their Stainmaster campaign.

Some pioneers choose to exit during this stage rather than face the price wars and spending wars that often occur in the next stage, Competitive Turbulence. If you choose to be that type of pioneer, you need to have the ability to continuously develop new products or services and successfully launch them which usually means your organization must be fast and flexible.

If you are a fast follower, then clearly your organization must be able to move quickly—otherwise you would be a slow follower. Moving

DuPont Stainmaster advertisement.

quickly means having an effective competitor information system and the ability to merchandise or sell broadly and in a short time. Often fast followers need to spend more to offset the entrenched position of the pioneer and that requires commitment.

The more expensive way for fast followers to compete is by imitation. They need to reverse engineer (analyze) the strengths and weaknesses of their competitors' products or services. Develop comparable products or services. Then use distribution and communications resources to saturate the market and out-muscle the competitors. Imitators also should have a legal staff expert in intellectual property law.

An imitation strategy can make sense when the pioneer continues to skim or is otherwise slow to go after the entire market. Large organizations also use imitation strategies when they think they can outspend smaller competitors and when their brand gives them special advantage with the target market.

Fast followers can also win with an innovation strategy. They improve the product or service beyond what the pioneer continues to produce. Such organizations understand customers' needs better than their competitors and also understand the weaknesses of their competitors' products or services. They communicate to the target customers a brand position that is superior to those of their competitors.

A German company developed a liquid laundry detergent that was superior to many powders on the market. They spent a lot of effort educating customers to the benefits of the liquid detergent. There was only one problem—the cap on their bottle leaked. A second company entered the market—their cap did not leak.

While the first company was the pioneer and market leader, that lasted only a short while. As customers discovered the leaking cap, they switched to the competitor's brand. The first company never fixed their cap and, in a short while, they were no longer prominent in the market. Pioneers must continually improve their product and fast-followers must always search for where the pioneering brand is vulnerable.

COMPETITIVE TURBULENCE STAGE

Market segmentation begins early in the competitive life cycle but is in full bloom during the Competitive Turbulence stage because customers get smarter and more demanding as to what they want and your competitors give it to them. There are many direct competitors in this stage and all their product or service offerings tend to be the same, leading to price wars and shake-out.

The key to your winning the Competitive Turbulence stage is targeting—your branding strategies must target the most attractive segments and your efforts focus on them.

To succeed with segmentation, you must understand the different bundles of benefits sought by customers and which groups of customers want which groups of benefits. At the same time as you are trying to identify and target different segments, you must also contain your costs by standardizing your product or service as much as you can. If you are not careful, pursuing many segments can increase your costs to unprofitable levels.

Issuers of credit cards understand market segmentation very well. They issue cards for many uses and for many income levels. At the same time, they have operating systems that allow them to share many costs while at the same time focus on many different target customers. Their problem is having a clear brand position.

For many years, MasterCard was losing ground to Visa. During this time frame, they were using many brand positions such as the "Future of Money" while Visa had a consistent campaign based on the tagline "Everywhere you want to be"—a strong functional benefit. When MasterCard launched their "Priceless" campaign, they found their brand voice and were able to connect an emotional benefit to their brand. Visa replied with a new campaign "Life Takes Visa," a logical build on their prior brand position. The story continues.

Visa and MasterCard advertisements over time.

MOUNTAIN DEW

The rejuvenation of Mountain Dew began in the mid 1980s. PepsiCo, the parent company of Mountain Dew, conducted research that confirmed their suspicions that Mountain Dew was not thought of as an urban or national brand but as a suburban or rural brand. When you say "Mountain Dew," the ad that most people still recall is a teenaged boy swinging on a rope across a water-filled quarry somewhere in what seems to be North Carolina—a brand position known as "Carolina cool." That was a memorable ad but did not do much for the new, edgier, urban position that Pepsi wanted for Mountain Dew.

Pepsi management set out to change that. They gave the Mountain Dew manager *seven* years to reposition the beverage for a hipper and more urban segment. In many companies, seven years is an eternity. Many managers who hear the Mountain Dew story are amazed that Pepsi had the patience (and the wisdom) to develop a seven-year strategy. The brand programs were developed each year but the target market and positioning were held constant over that period.

That was accomplished with a carefully designed communications campaign that continually moved the position of Mountain Dew toward a much edgier position but never tried to move it so far in one year that people would not find the ads credible.

The water sports became extreme sports and the tone of the ads became much more hip. The repositioning ads were run from the late 1980s to the mid-1990s. Every year new ads were made—-they didn't do seven years of creative work in advance. What they did do was establish the brand position very clearly and select the target market very clearly. Then they made sure that every year their communications strategy was on target and they kept moving the brand.

Mountain Dew video advertisements over time.

In the Mountain Dew campaign, if you were to see the first ad and the last ad from the repositioning campaign, my guess would be that you would say, "How did they do that?" However, if you look at a representative ad from each year, you will see an evolutionary change in the brand—almost like a strobe light film of a flower blooming. In these seven years of Mountain Dew spots, the locations change, the type of people change, the trade dress —the packaging changes, the music changes, the situations change, everything changes—but never so much as to lose the connection with the brand. Because the changes in communications were evolutionary rather than revolutionary, the brand was moved over a period of seven years—and was a major rejuvenation success.

Mountain Dew became the number three soft drink among their target segment, trailing only Coca-Cola and Pepsi-Cola.

Source: Anne Glover, "Rejuvenating Brand Equity," Talk at Building and Managing Brands Program, Columbia University, 1994.

Maturity Stage

Competitors often consolidate during the Mature stage. Now customers are very knowledgeable about the product or service and may view their purchase decision as routine.

> **You must retain your current customers by reinforcing your brand values but you must also attract new customers by finding what may be subtle differences versus your competitors.**

During the Mature stage, it is often difficult to increase perceived value to your customers. Therefore, you must pay special attention to your costs, using process engineering to reduce them without sacrificing benefits of importance to your customers.

Any differences in your product or service may have a large impact in the market.

A large part of the U.S. auto insurance industry is very much like a commodity business where lowest price wins. Both GEICO and Progressive insurance companies have followed brand strategies that still utilize price but couple it with superior service. For example, Progressive sends a van to where an accident occurs and settles the claim then. GEICO reviews the cost of your current policy and advises you of cheaper rates.

Rather than accept a commodity position, both companies found ways to differentiate themselves in terms of service. Both these companies have approximately doubled their shares over the last 10 years.

DECLINE STAGE

The reason the competitive life cycle declines is that a new product or service emerges that is more effective than the existing technology at meeting customers' needs.

During the Decline stage, your brand must be sufficiently stretchable so that you can move to the emerging technology.

To succeed in the Decline stage, clearly you must know you are in the Decline stage. You must monitor any possible new products or services that may affect your sales performance. Costs are usually critical in the latter stages of the life cycle so you must have managers who are cost-administrators. They reduce costs and do not over invest in branding, marketing, or design activities. All operations need to be efficient.

For the product or service in decline, objectives are often cash flow ("harvesting") or exiting without loss.

Often of more importance than succeeding during the Decline stage is being prepared to succeed in the next life cycle. *If* you want to stay with your customers, you must move to the new technology and hopefully your brand will stretch to that new technology. While laptop computers were entering the market, Smith-Corona was advertising a portable word-processor.

There have been a number of brands that are dominant in a technology but have faced difficulties moving to a new technology in the minds of customers. In many countries Kodak is synonymous with

Smith Corona laptop word processor advertisement.

film. That is a powerful position while film is being sold—less helpful when digital cameras are becoming popular. Of course, Kodak does sell many digital cameras. The issue is not whether Kodak can make or sell a digital camera but whether or not people think of Kodak when they want to buy a digital camera.

In the 1990s, Kodak advertisements displayed digital technology and included the tag line, "Take pictures further." However, poor financial results in the mid-1990s killed that campaign and Kodak fired many of their communications people. Since then, Kodak has developed promising new advertising campaigns such as "Share Moments, Share Life," to try to broaden the associations of the Kodak brand to include digital forms of imaging.

How important are these branding efforts? Very important. During one five-year interval, some publicly available brand equity estimates suggested that the value of the Kodak brand fell U.S.$7 billion—a loss of about half the brand's value. Managing their brand remains a crucial concern for Kodak.

An example more dramatic than Kodak is Polaroid—the company that invented instant photography and was synonymous with instant photography stopped producing instant film in 2008. They had made efforts to sell digital cameras but their brand was so strongly connected to instant photography that their ability to move to other products was seriously impaired.

Managing through the Competitive Life Cycle—Travel Agent Example

Suppose you own a small travel agency, catering to families and some businesses in your area. Your benefit advantage is convenience.

An office of a national chain travel agency opens in your town. They quote lower prices. Now you need to focus on the personalized service you deliver derived from your long-time knowledge of your clients.

Internet travel services increase in popularity. At the same time airlines also aggressively persuade their customers to book their flights directly online and cut your commissions. Online air travel booking is especially effective with business travelers who do not require much advice.

You decide to refocus your marketing to vacationers where your personal advice may be more valuable. You still need to contend with the Internet travel services who continue to add more value-added information on their sites.

The competitive life cycle is an unending story. You need to monitor customer needs and competitors constantly.

CONCLUSION

Each stage of the competitive life cycle calls for different kinds of branding strategies (see Exhibit 14.4). During the Introduction stage, benefits relevant to a customer are communicated through the salesforce and media. The Rapid Growth stage is the time when these benefits are wired to the brand because the functional benefits will likely be imitated during the Competitive Turbulence stage. Products and services in the Mature stage may have little functional differentiation but, hopefully, have great brand distinction. During the Decline stage, even a great brand may not survive if its technology is obsolete. You need to keep evolving your branding strategy so it is always optimal for your competitive conditions.

Exhibit 14.4 Competitive Life Cycle Stage and Branding Strategy

Stage	Introduction	Rapid Growth	Competitive Turbulence	Maturity	Decline
Key Characteristic	Competitor is old technology	Direct competitors enter	Segments emerge	Purchase routine	Competitor is new technology
Branding Strategy	Educate customer as to value	Differentiate from competitor	Target market segments	Reinforce and differentiate brand position	Associate brand with need*

*Must be done in early stages of the life cycle.
Source: "Arrow Guide—Managing through the Competitive Life Cycle," The Arrow Group, Ltd.®, New York, 2008. Used with permission.

III

BRANDING ON A
SMALL SCALE

15

BRANDING FOR
ENTREPRENEURS

Many entrepreneurs do not understand the power of branding and why one of their most important early tasks is to build their brand. For most organizations, their brand or reputation is their most important single asset.

Entrepreneurs must be thinking about building their brand even *before* they receive funding and make their business ideas reality. Their brand is their presence in their customers' minds and if they have no brand, they have no presence in the marketplace.

Brand-building must begin immediately with the start of the business. To build a successful brand takes time—perhaps five or six years—and the sooner one begins, the sooner one will obtain the returns from a well-designed and well-communicated brand.

In this chapter, you learn how an entrepreneur needs to think about his or her brand.

NEED FOR A BRAND

As an entrepreneur, you have many things on your mind. Is my business idea good enough? Can I obtain financing? Where will I locate? Will I use the Internet? Who should I hire? How can I put together a business plan?

With all those important questions seeking your attention, it is sometimes difficult to think of developing your brand. Selecting a brand requires reflection and thought and building a brand requires patience, discipline, and time. Often branding is overlooked in the excitement and chaos of the start-up period.

Not spending time thinking about your brand when you are beginning your business may cost you a lot more time—and money—later.

Beginning your brand-building early helps your business in two ways:

1. You save money and time on your brand-building because you make use of all your customer contacts from the very start. When you begin your business, you will be marketing your business—you might as well make sure all your marketing efforts support your brand from the beginning. That will help build your brand more quickly.
2. You save money and effort by not having to develop or change your brand position later. In particular, if your early marketing activities do not build a clear brand position, you will need eventually to do that brand-building work. Even more difficult, if your early marketing activities have somehow created a perception of your brand that you do not want, then you will have to undo that brand impression and then build the brand position that you do want.

As my friend, aphorist Ashleigh Brilliant has observed, it costs money to make money but it shouldn't cost more than you make so any way you can save is important.

Branding allows you to leverage the position of your venture to a wide variety of audiences—not only customers but also the financial community and others whom you may wish to impress favorably. It is never too early to begin thinking about your branding.

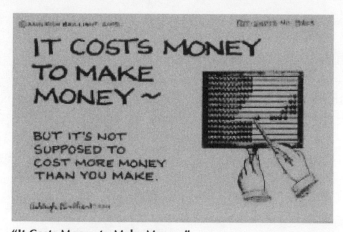

"It Costs Money to Make Money."
Illustration courtesy of Ashleigh Brilliant, © 2008 Ashleigh Brilliant.

Because building a brand requires consistency over time, you should start your brand-building when you start your company. In particular, you should decide on your brand position when you are developing your business plan.

You should start your brand-building when you start your company.

Associations are strong when there is a quick connection between the identifier and the attributes. For an entrepreneur, this is a major challenge. Because the entrepreneur is probably starting a company not yet known, they must develop the associations for their brand.

Brand Strategies for Start-Ups

The brand strategy for a start-up depends on when you start up and consequently what type of competitors you are facing. The competitive circumstances differ depending on when you enter the market and that will affect the type of strategy you should assemble. In Chapter 14, when we discussed managing your brand over time, we looked at how a brand strategy must change over time due to changing competitive conditions. Now we are looking at how those changing conditions determine the type of strategy you need to *enter* a market.

Time of entry not only affects the type of start-up strategy used, it also defines the type of skills an entrepreneur needs to succeed. If you want to enter a market in the Introduction stage, you will need a number of ideas. Only a small fraction of ideas for new products or services succeed so many ideas are required to deliver one success. (Of course, all you need is that one success.) An effective pioneer knows how to educate customers as to why their solution best solves the customer's problem. And pioneers are fast—otherwise someone else will get to the market before they do.

Often the Rapid Growth stage is where the eventual winner emerges. Pioneer entrepreneurs or fast-follower entrepreneurs are skilled at counter punching. They continually evolve their ideas for products or services and make sure that their brand is differentiated in the customer's mind versus those of their competitors.

If you enter in the Competitive Turbulence stage, you will often face a price war among the existing competitors. The key for entrepreneurs at this stage is a very tight focus on customer targets and the ability to keep costs low.

Whenever you enter a market and whatever the competitive circumstances, your product or service must have a *benefit advantage*—something you can provide the customer better than anyone else and something the customer wants (see Chapter 6). An entrepreneur must believe that their product or service fills a need in the marketplace. That belief may be based on marketing research but it may also be based on a hunch.

Whenever you enter a market, you need a benefit advantage.

Components of the Entrepreneur's Brand Plan

To build a strong brand, one needs a plan (Exhibit 6.2). An entrepreneur's business plan needs to include plans for activities such as financing, staffing, facilities, operations, marketing, and sales but it most certainly should include a brand plan.

The brand plan for a start-up consists of the same four basic components discussed in Chapter 6: Business Objectives, Target Market, Positioning, and Programs. Each needs to be considered over time, for example, for each quarter of the annual business plan:

1. *Business objectives:* What financial returns are expected and when? These objectives should be the same as set forth in the business plan. Most entrepreneurs know these very well.

2. *Target market:* On what customers will efforts be focused? They should be the same target customers as described in the marketing plan. For example, if you are opening a restaurant, you might target young singles or you might target family groups.

3. *Positioning:* What will be the key drivers that will persuade target customers to purchase? The brand position is related to the position stated in the marketing strategy but is usually more tightly defined. While many benefits of the product or service might be identified in the marketing plan, only a few benefits should be included in the brand position—those benefits that can be expected to be most effective with the customers.

    A restaurant might be known for its cuisine, its service, its selection of dishes, or its ambience. The brand position should be based on what their target customers want and what the restaurant does well.

    When entering a market, you will prefer to find a position where there are no existing brands. Unfortunately that may be difficult as the most attractive positions in the marketplace may already be occupied by existing competitors.

4. *Programs:* How will the brand position be communicated? What will be the identifiers—especially the name and logo? What specific communications methods will be employed? Mass media? Local media? Promotion? Public relations? Selling? Internet? When will they be employed?

All of these communications must be integrated. The target market and brand positioning guide the communications programs so that key customers will accurately understand the brand.

SELECTING THE TARGET MARKET

The starting point to develop the brand plan is the selection of a target market. Any entrepreneur needs to select a target market if their business is to succeed. If one has no market focus, then one's resources will be spread too thinly over customers. To persuade a customer to buy requires persistence as well as a good idea and persistence costs money. Choosing a target market is crucial to the success of a new venture.

First one lists possible *market segments*—these are groups of potential customers who are looking for the same benefits and who can be identified in some way. For example, suppose one were establishing a company to sell an innovative piece of office equipment. Possible market segments might be defined by size of company and industry.

Next one evaluates which of these possible market segments should receive attention. An entrepreneur should choose market segments that are *attractive*—that will potentially generate revenue and profits. However, they should also choose market segments where they have a strong *relative ability* to win the customers. Their relative ability determines the chances of winning the target market segment. (See Chapter 6 for more on segment selection.)

In the office equipment illustration, the entrepreneur might list all the possible segments such as small financial service companies or large manufacturing companies, then evaluate each possible market in terms of attractiveness and their relative ability to capture that market segment. Given the company is just starting up, it might be especially important to select just one or perhaps a few market segments so that the company's resources will not be spread over too many opportunities.

Valuable brands are built with *consistency* in brand position and consistency in communications. Some managers continuously change their brand position and brand communications. The result is confusion in the minds of their customers. Their customers do not know what their company or its products and services stand for. Consequently, the brand becomes *diffuse*—it does not stand for anything.

Being consistent requires *discipline* on the part of the entrepreneur. The entrepreneur must focus on the one or two key benefits that they will provide their customers. If they try to focus on too many benefits, the customers will not be able to apprehend all of that information. Unfortunately, most customers are not as dedicated to understanding and learning about a brand as is the owner of the business.

Consistent brand building requires discipline.

To build a successful brand, of course spending a lot of money helps. However, it is also possible to build a brand with a small budget—as long as one maintains consistency.

DETERMINING THE BRAND POSITION OF A START-UP

Whether to use a very specific brand name or a very general brand name is always an issue for a start-up.

The brand position should consist of one or two key benefits that the target customer cares about and that the entrepreneur can provide at a level to superior to those of their competitors. Only one or two benefits should be selected for the brand position because research has shown that most customers cannot recall a long list of benefits. If one tries to communicate several benefits, the customers may not remember any of those benefits or, if they do, it will be difficult to forecast which benefits they might remember.

That means if an entrepreneur is developing a housing complex, they should focus on the spaciousness of the apartments *or* their view *or* the service from the staff *or* the health club *or* the location *or* the financial terms—but not all of those benefits at once. Even if they are all mentioned in the brochure for the housing complex, the key brand benefits should be given more prominence.

The brand benefits should be important to the target customer, otherwise the benefits will not persuade him or her to make the purchase. The entrepreneur discovers which benefits are most important to the customer *by communicating with the target customer.* There is no substitute for talking with customers. Some of the largest new product disasters in the history of marketing such as Polavision and the RCA VideoDisc occurred because the products were designed with little input from customers.

The brand benefits should be benefits on which the entrepreneur's product or service is superior to those of competitors. In addition, that superiority should be *sustainable* over some period of time. A patented feature may provide a sustainable benefit. Location may provide a sustainable benefit. However, employees or operations might also be the basis for a sustainable benefit.

Finally, the brand benefits should usually not be benefits that are already part of a competitor's brand position. If a competitor has already built their brand on those benefits, then normally one can expect them to be able to retain them. If a brand of toothpaste is known to reduce the number of cavities, it is difficult to build a new brand on the same promise—*even* if the new brand is superior in fighting cavities. The exception is when the entrepreneur has made a major breakthrough, for example, in technology, such that it is obviously superior to all that it performs at a higher level than do existing brands.

Remember from Chapter 6 that your brand position is based on the one or two key benefits you are offering target customers to persuade them to do business with you rather than one of your target competitors. Your brand position is the heart of your business plan. It is the reason you expect to succeed and, consequently, also the reason you expect others to provide you with financial and other types of support.

If you are starting a software company, what makes your software special? Effectiveness? User-friendliness? Speed? Reliability? Whatever makes your software special will be the basis for your brand position.

If your software provides many benefits to your customer, then select the one or two benefits that are most important and—ideally—those benefits that no one else provides as well as you do.

EXTERNAL BRAND COMMUNICATIONS

External brand communications are communications directed toward the target customers and any other group of importance to the company such as investors and suppliers.

As always, the main principle of external communications is *consistency*—consistency over time and over audiences.

If the brand message is constantly changing, then the brand position will be destabilized. However, that does not mean that you would never change a brand position over time. As an entrepreneur sees his or her company grow, it may well happen that he or she wishes to alter his or her brand position. The way to change a brand position, however, is to make the changes gradually so they appear consistent with the current brand changes. Abrupt changes in brand positions confuse customers—the customers also may not find abrupt changes to be credible.

For example, as described in Chapter 14, the brand position of the soft drink Mountain Dew was changed gradually over a seven-year period from a relatively bland rural image to a much edgier and hipper, urban image. In no single year was the change in brand position so large it was not believable, but over seven years, the brand position was moved a considerable distance. In contrast, Thom McAn shoes tried to change their brand position within months and were notably unsuccessful.

Consistency refers not only to time but to audiences. If different brand messages are directed to different customers, it can work only if the customers are "partitioned"—that means they do not see the messages aimed at others and see only the messages aimed at them. For example, younger customers and older customers may read quite different magazines and therefore might represent partitioned markets if you are advertising in magazines. If a specific customer sees different messages about the brand, then that can destabilize the brand by blurring the brand position in the minds of the customers exposed to the different brand messages.

As regards spending on external communications, clearly more is better. However, many entrepreneurs have small budgets and cannot afford to advertise in media such as television or national magazines. They should consider using some form of guerrilla marketing (Chapter 16). Guerrilla marketing makes use of less expensive communications such as handbills, business cards, circulars, posters, customer promotions, public relations, local radio, local newspapers—anything that will generate word-of-mouth and interest in their product or service.

> **Whatever media are used, the message should always be consistent to customers in a specific target market.**

SANDWICHES OF THE WORLD

The launch of the book, *Sandwiches of the World* took place in the Atrium of Trump Tower. Chefs from well-known New York City restaurants assembled to sign next to their recipes. The Trumpwich, developed by Chris Devine, resident chef at Trump Tower, was one of the creations featured in the book. A portion of the book sales was donated to The Children's Storefront, a tuition-free school in Harlem.

Source: Donald J. Trump, "Giving Back," *Trump University Magazine,* December 2007.

COMMUNICATING INTERNALLY

Employees must understand what the brand stands for and why it is important to the company. In a small organization, the entrepreneur can personally inform their employees. In larger organizations, it may be necessary to prepare materials—often called a *brand book*—that describe the brand, the key benefits in the brand position, and why building and maintaining the brand is crucial to the company. Companies such as GE, Caterpillar, and Harley-Davidson maintain their brand positions with the help of their brand books.

Especially in start-up organizations that provide services, in the eyes of the customers, the employees *are* the organization's brand. They must "live" the brand.

Monitoring the Brand

It is true that "if you can't measure it, you can't manage it." Branding efforts are like any other effort in a company; they must be examined over time.

A common measure of branding results is brand awareness. That is the percentage of target customers who know of the brand name. However, usually brand awareness is not sufficient to properly evaluate the initial strength of a brand. You need to know the attributes that target customers associate with the brand (see Exhibit 3.1). If all the customers know is the name of your brand, typically that is not enough to persuade them to purchase. Customers need to know what your brand *stands for*—that is the power of the brand.

At a minimum, an entrepreneur should ask customers on a regular basis whether they have heard of their brand and, if so, what attributes they associate with the brand name. One would like to see that many of the target customers know the brand position. Such information can be collected in surveys, but also simply talking to one's customers and potential customers can provide useful brand monitoring information. See Chapter 22 for more suggestions as to how to monitor your brand's performance.

Brands and Raising Money

The marketing aspects of the brand plan consist of target market, brand position, and programs. Business objectives must be added to complete the brand plan. The entrepreneur's objectives depend on their assessment of competing products and services and the likely reception that customers will give to their product or service as well as the return they need to justify the pursuit of the venture. Constructing the business objectives is beyond what can be covered reasonably in this book. Please see *Trump University Entrepreneurship 101* (Hoboken, NJ: Wiley, 2006) for a discussion of setting financial objectives. However, a strong brand will certainly make attainment of those objectives more likely.

Conclusion

Often entrepreneurs skip over the brand plan because they think it is something that they can pursue later. That may be a mistake. Brands may take a long time to build, and the sooner one starts, the higher the chance of success. Starting early to build a brand may require less investment in the long run because there may be fewer competitors and more brand positions available. It is difficult and often expensive to take a brand position away from a competitor that has already fortified their position.

Developing the brand strategy helps the entrepreneur develop their overall business plan. If you cannot identify one or two key benefits that your product or service provides the target customer—as you must do to develop a brand plan—then there may not be demand for your product or service.

But above all, strong brands lead to higher revenue, profits, and cash flow. The sooner the entrepreneur builds the brand, the sooner they receive those higher returns.

16

GUERRILLA BRANDING:
BRANDING FOR SMALL
BUSINESSES

Many small businesses fail because they do not use the powerful branding and marketing principles used by the most successful companies in the world. Often a small business such as a printer or a real estate agent or an automobile repair service simply opens their doors and hopes that customers will find them. In a recent survey of small businesses, 55 percent of the respondents thought that they did not need much marketing since their products or services sold themselves (William J. Dennis Jr., *National Small Business Poll: Marketing Perspectives*, 2006, v. 6, n. 8).

Unfortunately, many small businesses fail because that is not how it works. Of course, some customers will find their ways to small businesses by chance and those businesses may succeed. But why leave matters to chance when you can increase the probability that your business will succeed by putting the fundamental and proven strategic ideas of branding to use?

This chapter provides ideas as to how to build strong brands with limited budgets.

Small Businesses and Branding

There are two major reasons why owners of small businesses may not utilize the full power of branding:

1. *The owners may think of branding as consisting of tactics and ignore the strategic aspects of branding.* Often people think of branding as advertising or promotion or possibly public relations. These are important branding tools but they are *tactics*. They are used to implement a branding strategy. A strategy without tactics is simply hopeful thoughts. However, tactics without strategy are actions without purpose.

2. *The owners may believe that branding is too expensive.* Most businesses do not have the branding budgets of Toyota, IBM, or Tata. For those companies, it is especially important that they concentrate their efforts through a clear branding strategy. In addition, small businesses are flexible and have the ability to employ *guerrilla branding* to implement their branding strategies inexpensively but effectively.

Guerrilla Branding Strategy

As you know from Chapter 6, all branding strategies include four major components: Target Markets, Business Objectives, Positioning, and Programs (Exhibit 6.2). Target markets consist of the customers on which you want to focus. Business objectives are what you want from your business—typically stated as revenue or profits. Positioning refers to the key benefits you provide your target customers. Programs are the tactics used to implement the strategy and include advertising, promotion, pricing, and distribution.

A guerrilla branding strategy is similar to any branding strategy with one major difference—the resources available are limited so that care must be taken as to where effort will be placed. That places even more importance on the two components that are central to all brand strategies: targeting and positioning. Targeting *concentrates* your branding efforts while positioning *coordinates* your branding efforts.

Guerrilla Branding Targets

For guerrilla branding, targeting markets is especially crucial. When you have limited resources, you must be sure that you *concentrate* your efforts as efficiently and as effectively as possible. For example, if you open a restaurant, do you want to focus on families or on single individuals? If you open a health club, do you want to focus on younger or older clients? If you open a carpentry business, do you want to focus on indoor or outdoor work? If you open a building cleaning service, do you want to focus on offices or homes?

Without a clear target market, smaller businesses do not concentrate their efforts on specific markets and may spread their resources too thin. Instead of focusing on target customers and building loyalty among them, they may obtain occasional purchases from customers who know them only slightly and have no reason to return.

If there are no clear customer targets, branding tactics may be wasted. The choice of target markets guides the tactics such as how, where, and when you communicate with your customers. A dental clinic focused on children might advertise in magazines read by parents while a dental clinic focused on young adults might advertise in publications concerned with leisure and entertainment.

If there are no clear customer targets, then branding tactics may be wasted.

Smaller businesses without target markets may accept all kinds of business. By doing that, they confuse their customers and diffuse their brand image.

GUERRILLA BRAND POSITIONING

Your benefit advantage—the reason your target customers should buy from you—is the heart of your branding strategy. Choosing a clear and easily understandable benefit advantage as your brand position is the first step to building a strong business and a strong brand. Your brand position coordinates all your brand efforts so that they reinforce the same message over time. If the position is not clear or is not communicated well, both internally and externally, it is difficult to have a consistent brand message.

It is always tempting to tell customers every good thing possible about your product or service. If you try that, the consequence is that your customers may remember very little about what is good about your product or service that is important to them. You need to choose carefully what you will tell them about your brand.

GUERRILLA BRANDING TACTICS

Once you have chosen your target markets and determined your positioning, you are ready to implement your brand strategy with your guerrilla tools (see Exhibit 16.1).

Remember how strong brands are built. *Consistency in your branding efforts—over time and over everything that you do.* That is true for large and for small organizations. Every contact you have with the target customer should repeat and reinforce the brand position. That means for consistent branding, your staff must also have a clear understanding of your brand strategy so their actions will support the strategy. All those in your organization involved in implementing your branding strategy must know your target markets and brand positioning.

Exhibit 16.1   Guerrilla Branding Tools

Name and logo
Advertising tag line
Mailers
Brochures
Circulars
Miniposters
Trading leads with related businesses
Newsletters
Personal letters
Personal telephone calls
Employee contacts with customers
Business cards
Stationery
Signs—outdoors
Signs—indoors
Posters
Banners
Promotions
Coupons
Giveaways
Web site
Blog
Local newspaper ads
Local radio ads
Telephone directory ads
Newspaper articles
Magazine articles
Radio interviews
Speeches before local groups
Attending trade shows or conferences
Support for community organizations

Source: "Arrow Guide—Guerrilla Branding," The Arrow Group, Ltd.®, New York, 2008. Used with permission.

GUERRILLA BRANDING IDENTIFIERS

Your identifiers are all those images that you use to make customers aware of your business. Your identifiers include the name of your business, but also may include a symbol or logo or a tag line used in your advertising.

Small businesses can use the same techniques that large companies use. Select a name that is linked to your positioning—what makes your business special to your target customers. If your laundry service prides itself on removing any stain, then find a name that connotes that. If your plumbing service is always ready to help, use a name that indicates you are always available. You may find it worthwhile to hire a graphics designer—maybe even a student—to make you a logo. Money spent on logo design is worthwhile because you should expect to use your logo for a long time.

Your identifiers should be consistent. Use the same type font, the same color ink, the same logo everywhere. Do not change your identifiers over time unless you have a very sound reason and you are prepared to start investing all over again in building your brand name.

Keep your identifiers consistent.

Suggestions

- Your name should describe a bit about what you offer. Don't just say Jones Flowers—say Jones Fresh Flowers.
- Design a logo—it need not be fancy but should communicate what you do.
- Develop a tag line—Jones Fresh Flowers—Bringing Beauty to the County for Years.
- Keep the colors and the typeface the same in all your communications.

GUERRILLA BRANDING SERVICE

All your employees represent your brand. You need to check your contact points with customers to be sure that your employees' actions are consistent with your brand position. For example, if your store sells clothing for children and your brand position consists of caring about children's well-being, then your store salespeople should reflect that in their attitudes and behavior with customers.

Suggestions

- Make clear to all your customer contact employees that how they treat customers is important to building the brand.
- Provide training for your customer contact employees especially as regards listening and answering the telephone.
- Adjust your hours for the convenience of your customers.
- Consider using an 800 number if it would be more convenient for your customers.
- Provide small thoughtful touches that your customers appreciate such as parking spaces reserved for them or fresh coffee in the waiting area.
- Keep your business space well-organized and neat in appearance.

Guerrilla Branding Communications

All your advertising needs to be targeted toward your target customers. Guerrilla branding communications cannot overwhelm with volume—they achieve their goals through focus.

Guerrilla communications clearly state your brand position—your key benefits—and how to contact you. There is no need to waste space on extraneous information that will only dilute your primary message.

Use every method of communications that you can afford. But make sure that you give each communications method sufficient resources so that it will have an effect. Personalize your communications as much as possible. Addressing your customers personally is a major advantage a small business has over a large business and you should be sure to exploit it.

Use every method of communications that you can afford.

Inexpensive media include one- or two-page flyers that you can use as mailers, hand-outs, or post on bulletin boards or in windows as mini-posters. You should view your business cards and stationery as mini-posters as well. They should employ your identifiers and provide the target customer with as much information about your services as possible without creating a cluttered appearance. Use both sides of your business cards if necessary.

Do not neglect your signs. They are often the first impression a customer receives of your business. Again, they should employ your identifiers but also—if possible—give a brief reference to your benefit advantage. These references need not be subtle. A childcare center might show happy children and a mattress store might show someone comfortably asleep. Besides signs, use anything that might acceptably attract attention to your business like banners or balloons for a toy store or posters for a cinema.

Find ways to stay in touch with your customers. Collect their addresses and keep them on file—perhaps ask for your customers' business cards. Trade leads with related businesses—a caterer may exchange leads with a banquet hall, for example. If possible, send them a newsletter with advice. For example, a health club might send a newsletter with exercise tips and a motorcycle repair service might provide advice on maintaining a motorcycle.

When developing your guerrilla branding communications strategy, you may find it helpful to find out where your customers get information—bulletin boards, radio stations, mailers, wherever. Then try to utilize those communications channels. Keep in mind that there are a great variety of ways to communicate with your customers— many that can be much more precisely targeted than the mass media.

Guerrilla branding can include some of the less costly media such as local newspapers, local radio, or telephone directories. If your customers are online, then perhaps a web site or a blog will be effective for you. However, whatever media are used, they must be focused on your target customers and they must consistently communicate your benefit advantage. While not a small business, Altoids mints used some of the principles of guerrilla branding when building their brand. Rather than utilizing expensive broadcast media, they employed many outdoor ads and novel media such as postcards to communicate their message. Their media reinforced their irreverent message.

Altoids advertisements.

Photo credit: Don Sexton. Photos courtesy of Don Sexton.

Suggestions

- Inventory all the points of contacts you have with your customers or potential customers and make sure your brand identifiers are visible in all those places.
- Your signs should be easy to see, make clear what you do, and show your contact information.
- Print a number of one-page advertisements that you can use as mailers, circulars, signs, mini-posters, inserts, and handouts.
- Use your stationery as your representative—it is. Don't cut costs.
- Treat your business cards as small billboards. Don't cut costs on them. Use both sides of the card if necessary and provide reasons why customers should buy from you.
- Find reasons to send customers or clients personal messages—on holidays, their birthdays, or on other occasions such as when they need their furnace inspected or their teeth checked.
- Employ a newsletter—either hard copy or digital. Be sure it has information of value to your customers. A dive shop might provide SCUBA equipment tips and information on upcoming diving trips and courses.
- Find unusual media such as videos, DVDs, banners, balloons, sidewalk displays, searchlights, skywriting, or tethered blimps.

- Use Yellow Pages ads. In addition to your contact information, be sure to include reasons why the customer should buy from you.
- Consider using mass media but keep in mind that some print and broadcast advertising can be purchased as *remnants*—advertising spaces or times that are unsold and can be purchased at the last minute at relatively low rates.

GUERRILLA BRANDING PROMOTIONS

Offer promotions (although always be sure to check on their legality). Contests can create excitement and interest in your business. Have open houses where customers can obtain advice. Use coupons or inexpensive giveaways to attract customers. If you run a beauty salon, offer a free introductory service during a day when typically you have little business. Make sure your promotions are themed to be consistent with your brand positioning.

Suggestions

- Organize customer groups and develop relationships with your customers. Huggies sends personalized letters and magazines on baby care to women who are pregnant. In my town, a children's clothing store uses mailing lists of their customers and potential customers to support a group interested in parenting issues.
- Give inexpensive items that will remind customers and potential customers of your products or services. Examples include t-shirts, caps, or paperweights, but perhaps you can be more creative. One consultant I know gives out balls which, when tilted, provide answers to questions that can be seen through a window in the ball.
- Employ contests. A health club might give away memberships and a massage service free massages. Hold the contest with local nonprofit groups so that you benefit in terms of public relations as well.

- Focus contests on your brand position—perhaps ask entrants to give examples of your brand position as they have experienced it. You may be able to use those later (with permission) as testimonials.

GUERRILLA BRANDING PUBLIC RELATIONS

Do not overlook public relations, which has the potential to provide you with considerable marketing impact at low cost—just what guerrilla branding is about. Articles about your business provide you valuable exposure but do require effort. You need to know the deadlines of publications and send them press releases in their preferred format. You should try to be in touch with representatives of your local media. Also give talks and otherwise support local organizations. Attend trade fairs or conferences.

Suggestions

- Make sure your press releases are in the form desired and arrive well before deadlines.
- Create a list of e-mail addresses so you can distribute your press releases digitally.
- Develop a first-name relationship with your local newspaper and radio station reporters. If appropriate, have lunch or coffee with them.
- Print reprints of articles about your business and use them as mailers or circulars.
- Take an active role in your community. If affordable, sponsor local teams.
- Show the work of local artists. Contribute goods or services to local not-for-profit organizations.
- Be active in local associations. Give presentations.
- Be known as the local expert on matters relating to attributes of your brand. For example, if you are a contractor, be known for the use of new building techniques or, if you are a caterer, be known for certain types of cuisine.

On Riverside Drive, near the West Side Highway in Manhattan is Trump Place—a series of luxury condominiums and rental units developed by the Trump Organization. As you drive south on the West Side Highway, you will see a sign: "Henry Hudson Beautification Project—Donald J. Trump—Adopt-a-Highway." The sign reinforces the Trump name in a very positive fashion. In addition, it announces Trump Place that you see seconds after passing the sign.

Donald J. Trump Adopt-A-Highway sign.
Photo credit: Don Sexton. Photo courtesy of Don Sexton.

GUERRILLA BRANDING ON THE INTERNET

Remember that all communications with customers should have the same look and feel, including your web site and e-mail messages. When you have a small budget, it is especially important that all communications reinforce each other.

Suggestions

- Develop a web site that communicates your brand position. Don't forget to include your contact information, including an easy-to-use e-mail service.
- Set up a blog.
- Get listed on free directories relevant to your brand.
- Manage your search engine placement.
- E-mail a brand-reinforcing newsletter to your customers and prospective customers.
- Use chat rooms.

GUERRILLA BRANDING RESEARCH

The main advantage small organizations have versus large organizations is that they are usually closer to their customers. You can use those relationships to learn what you need to do to improve your brand and get their business.

Suggestions

- Try to find out how satisfied your customers are with your products or services and see if they have any suggestions for improvements.
- Ask friends if they know what your brand stands for and whether how they are treated is consistent with your brand.
- Conduct informal focus groups—where you invite 5 or 6 of your customers or potential customers to discuss your products or services over coffee or snacks.
- Conduct a survey focused on your brand position among current and potential customers.

CONCLUSION

Branding does not have to be expensive to be effective—it does need to be targeted and relentlessly consistent. Guerrilla branders know the customers they want and know the reasons those customers should be buying from them. All their marketing efforts are guided by those principles.

While it is always desirable to have a large branding budget, most small businesses cannot afford to spend a lot on branding. That is why they might utilize creative guerrilla branding tactics that exploit their proximity to the customer. Often these are tactics that large companies cannot emulate.

17

Branding the Individual: Your Personal Brand

You are a brand. The only question is whether you want to manage your brand or not.

If you choose not to manage your brand, then others will manage it for you. However, whether those others are your friends and relatives or whether they are your competitors or your rivals at work, be assured that they do not know your brand the way you do, nor do they care about your brand the way you care about it.

All the principles of branding apply equally well to your brand as they do to a product or a service—with a few important differences. This chapter shows you how to use branding ideas to develop your personal brand.

Why Develop Your Personal Brand?

Suppose you have a small business—perhaps a realty office or a contracting business or a clothing store. Maybe you spend a lot of time prospecting for customers and then trying to sell them your products or services.

Wouldn't you prefer customers to come to you? And then you have the opportunity to accept them or not? That can happen with a strong personal brand.

Suppose you work in an organization—perhaps an insurance company or a university or a hospital. Maybe you watch others being moved past you in their careers.

Wouldn't you prefer managers to seek you out for promotion? That can happen with a strong personal brand.

A strong personal brand will not cover up incompetence. As with any brand, there has to be value backing up the brand position. You must be able to deliver your brand promise. A strong personal brand will help place you in the top of your customers' or clients' minds—or even in the top of your bosses' mind. You will be more likely to be considered for new projects or for promotions.

For a business, a strong personal brand should lead to a more stable customer base and a steadier stream of customers. There is no more effective communications than word-of-mouth among your customers and potential customers and a strong personal brand encourages such activity.

A strong, personal brand will not solve all your problems. You will still need to work. But a strong, personal brand will free you up to do what you want instead of chasing potential customers and clients—hopefully they will chase or at least come looking for you.

A strong personal brand will not solve all your problems—you will still need to work.

WHEN SHOULD YOU DEVELOP A PERSONAL BRAND?

A personal brand will have more impact the more your personal brand attributes might be expected to affect your business. In particular, if you have a small, personal service business such as a dental clinic, marketing research agency, or a beauty salon, your personal characteristics, as embodied in your brand, can be important brand attributes of your business.

Personal brands also can influence customers of businesses where advice and service are important dimensions of the customer experience. For example, an automobile dealership, clothing store, or florist all would benefit from a strong personal brand.

In business situations where there is considerable human interaction, research has shown that approximately 70 percent of customer satisfaction is due to human relationships (Valerie A. Zeithaml, Leonard L. Berry, and A. Parasuraman, *Delivering Quality Service*, New York: Free Press, 1990). Those are the situations where a personal brand can be expected to have significant effects on the performance of the business.

A personal brand makes an impersonal situation personal. Generally, people prefer to deal with people rather than faceless and nameless organizations. A personal brand gives a face and a name to your business.

Principles of Personal Branding

Branding principles apply to building a personal brand. In particular:

- You need to focus your branding efforts on the customers you most want.
- You must have a brand position. Your brand must stand for something—something that will appeal to your customers.
- You must be sure that all you do—actions and communications—is consistent with your brand position.
- You must have patience and commitment—branding always takes time.

BUILDING YOUR PERSONAL BRAND

To build a personal brand plan (Exhibit 6.2), you should take the following six steps:

1. Select your target customers.
2. Determine what appeals to your target customers.
3. Consider what distinguishes you from others.
4. Evaluate how your characteristics match up with what your target customers are looking for.

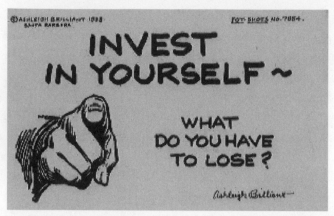

"Invest in Yourself." Illustration courtesy of Ashleigh Brilliant,
© 2008 Ashleigh Brilliant.

5. Describe your brand position.
6. Make clear your brand position through your actions and communications.

Select Your Target Customers Consider your current customers. Which ones purchase the most? Which are the most profitable? Which ones provide you the most referrals? You should want to keep these customers and find others like them. These are your target customers.

Note that it is all right not to want all your current customers. There are some customers who should be "fired" because they demand too much and pay too little. You want your personal brand to attract your target customers and, ideally, repel the customers you do not want.

You want to discover what it is that your target customers like about you and what you do. You can ask them directly what they like about you. Or you might ask them how they describe you to others. For clients that were referred to you, ask them how others described you to them and why they decided to call on you.

**What do your customers like about you
and what you do?**

While you are talking with customers, try to learn how they view the competitors. They may not wish to share those thoughts with you. If they don't, do not press the point. You do not want to get into a discussion of your competitors where you may have to give an opinion. That is dangerous territory—you never want to be tempted to say something negative about one of your competitors.

Whether your customers tell you about your competitors, you certainly have an idea of what they are like—what they are good at and what they are not so good at. You want to write those characteristics down so you can compare them to what you do well and not so well and which competitors might appeal to your target customers.

Your Personal Brand Audit   You need to train the spotlight on yourself and understand what might be the foundation attributes of your personal brand. For example, think of business situations where you have done well—what were the reasons for your success? Similarly, think of business situations, where you did not do so well—what were the reasons for your failure? What have you done that has led to successful and long-term relationships with your customers or clients?

Now think whether you can replicate what you did well and if that will appeal to your target customers.

What you are looking for are a few phrases that might capture your personal brand—especially if they describe characteristics that your customers want and that your competitors do not provide.

Your Brand Position   Your personal brand position should consist of only a few of your characteristics: reliable, punctual, thoughtful, creative, friendly, knowledgeable, flexible. Ideally, your brand position should consist of *one* characteristic but, in any case, no more than two or three.

The reason is the usual reason—your customers and potential customers will find it difficult to recall more than three characteristics about your personal brand and, if they do, they may not remember much about each of several characteristics. In addition, since this is your personal brand, if you claim too many favorable traits, people may simply not believe that you can be (or do) all those things. Parsimony is key to building an effective personal brand.

For example, if you are preparing a resume, you should target the resume to the position you are seeking. My students often ask me: "How many resumes should I have?" My answer: "As many resumes as the number of positions you are competing for." If your resume tries to show you can do anything—*even* if you can—the person reviewing your resume may not believe that any one of your many diverse skills is superior to those of a specialist.

Besides your key traits or attributes, your personal brand position should contain information that makes you special, such as your background, awards, special interests, personality, or lifestyle. These dimensions make you different from a company and give people ways to relate to you. For example, if you are a Scuba diver, find a way to mention that. It provides a way for people to engage you and for you to engage them.

Your personal brand position should make it clear why you are special.

Try to capture your personal brand in a few phrases. This description is what you will use to test your actions and communications for consistency. No customer may ever directly see the description of your brand position but they will know what it is indirectly through your actions and communications.

WYLAND

Wyland began building his brand by painting ocean-life murals on the walls of buildings.

The first was on the wall of a hotel in Laguna Beach in 1981. Since then he has painted more than 90 others. Today, he is the "world's foremost marine environmental artist," passionate about his art and passionate about the marine environment.

The first time I saw a Wyland wall was on the side of a hotel in Waikiki. It was an astonishing and spectacular sight. As a

---

Wyland Wall in Miami
Photo credit: Don Sexton. Photos courtesy of Don Sexton.

Scuba diver, the image had special meaning for me. My immediate reaction was, who did that? His signature was very clear and very easy to read and remember.

His public art propelled him to a position as an internationally known artist in just a few years. Today his images appear on a wide variety of merchandise in stores around the world, including fine art, gift products, books, and apparel.

As Wyland observed to Peter Montoya, "My brand is narrowly focused and widely focused on conservation and ocean issues." Always his brand is kept consistent—the signature is always one word, "Wyland," and his work always stands for "the ocean, marine life, and conservation."

Source: Peter Montoya, *The Brand Called You,* Tustin, CA: Personal Branding Press, 2005, pp. 161–163; and Wyland web site.

Implementing Your Personal Brand

Your personal brand is built with every contact you have with your customers. The branding programs for a personal brand may include:

- Your identifiers—name, logo, tag line
- Your appearance and that of your employees
- The appearance of your place of business
- The actions of you and your employees
- Business cards and stationery
- Brochures and similar materials
- Seminars
- Events
- Promotions
- Personal communications
- Public relations
- Web site, e-mail, blogs
- Calls on customers or potential customers
- Mass communications

All of these can reinforce each other. You should try to touch your target customers in as many ways as possible—use at least four or five ways. For example, you hold an open house at your beauty salon. You gather contact information from those attending and give them your brochure. You follow up with a short-term promotion for them to try your services. You e-mail them to announce your new stylist. Your blog provides them with updated information about your services. Multiple contacts increase the chances of their effect and the development of your personal brand.

Identifiers If you have a choice, name your company with your name (or even that of a relative, e.g., Wendy's). Giving your company the name of a real person underscores that your customers will be dealing with a person, not a faceless company. TruValue Hardware includes the name of their store operators in the name of each store—that personalizes each outlet. Which would you rather deal with—the Global XYZ Automobile Repair Corporation or Al and Barbara's Auto Repair?

Even if you are already using a name that is not your own, you may wish to consider changing it. If you do change it, be sure to contact personally your key customers to explain the reason for the change.

Your logo should be simple so that it is easily visible. Try to avoid clip-art solutions that anyone could use and try to find an image that will be unusual but memorable. If you operate an Italian restaurant, for example, do not use a common logo with plates or food but try to find an image that will make you stand apart from other similar restaurants.

Once you have an image in mind, you will likely find it worthwhile to hire a professional artist to render it unless you happen to have drawing skills. Restrict yourself to no more than two colors. Multiple-color logos are expensive to print.

Tag lines are short phrases that elaborate your brand—something like a subtitle. Tag lines are not essential but sometimes can help make your personal brand distinctive. Your tag line should be descriptive. Don't say, "J. Smith, Accountant." Say, "J. Smith, The Good News Accountant" or "J. Smith, The Real Estate Accountant."

Appearances When you meet someone for the first time, how do you begin to develop your opinion of them? Usually from their appearance. You may change your opinions later but that happens only if you have a continued relationship with that person. In a business situation, appearance can terminate the relationship before it begins.

Appearance includes personal appearance and, if customers visit your office, the appearance of your office. As regards personal appearance, the general rule is dress just a bit more formally than your customers. If they are in jeans, you should be business casual. If they are business casual, then you may need to be in regular business clothes.

Personal appearance considerations apply to you and all your employees.

Your office should also make an effective impression. Neat and businesslike, of course. In addition, placement of awards, certificates, letters of customer appreciation, photos of sponsored teams, artwork—all bolster your personal brand.

Actions   After appearance, people develop their initial opinions of others based on their actions. When dealing with your customers, manage their expectations. Do not promise what you cannot deliver—and then make excuses afterward. Rather, promise what you know you can deliver. Then if your performance is even better, your customer will be grateful.

Your day-to-day actions and those of your employees should support your personal brand. You should not have to be involved in every transaction and every activity and that is why it is important for your staff to know what your personal brand stands for and their role in building your brand. They should also understand why building the brand is critical to the success of the business. Suggestions for informing them about the brand are described in Chapter 23.

Business Cards, Stationery, and Brochures   Do not try to cut costs on business cards, stationery, and brochures. They communicate your brand and you need them to make an effective impression.

Business cards should display your distinctive logo, but also provide some information about what you do and why you are distinctive—"the acknowledged expert in real estate taxation." Stationery can also provide information that reinforces your brand. The tag line might be printed along the bottom of the page.

Do not cut costs on business cards, stationery, and brochures.

Your brochure should not be the typical three-fold black-and-white model that everyone has seen and that no one reads. Its appearance should be dramatic—perhaps strong colors or an unusual shape. Photos should be in color if at all possible and show you and your employees in action—not sitting at a desk but with clients or celebrating an award. Include in your brochure elements of your own personal story. For example, why you became an accountant or what are your proudest achievements. Include testimonials from clients that will reinforce your personal brand attributes.

Once you have developed your brochure, send a few copies to your current customers—one for themselves, the rest to give others. Send a copy to each of your potential customers and, if appropriate, find locations where you might leave supplies for people to find. For example, if you are a contractor, you might leave your brochures at hardware stores or at lumber yards.

Seminars and Events   Seminars obviously must focus on topics that people care about. To determine topics, think first about target markets. Financial advisors have information with potential appeal to many people but their seminars need to be focused on target markets—young couples or senior retirees, for example. Each target market will have different issues of concern and you should not try to mix them in one audience and tell them everything you know about everything. You need to focus your attention on one target market at a time.

Seminars can be recorded and the recordings used as giveaways or even provided to local broadcast stations for possible airing.

Events include trade shows and fairs. Events provide the chance for one-on-one contacts with customers—the type of opportunity you want to build your personal brand.

Both seminars and events are opportunities for beginning the relationship with your customers. Be sure to capture the contact information of attendees or visitors. You need to have your brochure ready and then—very important—follow up.

Promotions   Promotions include giveaways and contests. The theme for any promotion should be one that reinforces the main attributes of your personal brand. If you give away t-shirts, for example, the images or the sayings should be related to your personal brand. A local realtor uses photos of the two partners on all their promotional materials.

Personal Communications   Here is where your personal brand gives you a tremendous advantage over companies. As a person, you can connect to individuals—if you take the time. Whenever I travel, I stay in touch with customers by sending them personally written postcards from wherever I am—China, India, Europe. I am a painter and each year I send out holiday postcards featuring one of my paintings of New York City in the winter (see Exhibit 17.1). These are things that I can do but which would be very difficult for a corporation to do. All I need is to secure one new client to make these efforts worthwhile.

You can print postcards specific to your business—space for postage and an address label and information about your company on one side, more about your company and a white space on the other. Whenever you have an announcement or something you wish to tell your customers about, you can print it in the white space, then send out the cards. If you sign it and include a brief note, it makes the communication even more personal.

Public Relations   For personal branding, as for small business branding, public relations can be extraordinarily effective. The one problem with public relations is that you cannot count on it because reporters and editors or producers decide whether your information is newsworthy. Still, the more press releases you send out, the higher the chance that your news will be published or aired.

You can increase those odds by making sure you understand the format for press releases desired by the media and know their deadlines. If you can develop associations with the local reporters or editors or producers, that can also help get you heard.

Internet   If your target customers can be expected to be online, you need to have a web site. Online participation does vary by age group

Exhibit 17.1   Don's Holiday Card

management development/training/consulting/conference speakers

Wishing you a joyous Holiday season

and a New Year of peace and happiness.

Don Sexton

White Street in Snow © 2002
Don Sexton
31" × 25"/79 cm × 64 cm
Ink and oil pastel

Source: Donald E. Sexton, "White Street in Snow," New York, © 2002. Used with permission.

and by country but, for many businesses, a web site is necessary. In developing a web site, you need to decide what you want it to do for you. The most basic web site provides information about services and contact information. You need to decide if you wish to move to the next steps of supporting transactions and obtaining customer information.

Once you have decided on your objectives for the web site, unless you are skilled in web site development, you should hire someone who is. They can make the site appear professional and attractive. However, you should provide continuous input to ensure that the web site supports your personal brand position, for example, by including statements from you and information about you.

E-mail messages are yet another way to communicate personally to your customers and clients. Ideally, each message should seem like a conversation with the individual. If possible, try to include one or two phrases that indicate the message is not a general broadcast—perhaps mentioning the last time you saw the person or inquiring about a vacation or other personal matter. The messages should have content that is of value to the recipient. If you operate a dive shop, then you might let your customer know about a new dive site you have found. If you are an accountant, you might mention a new tax ruling. If you are a realtor, you might discuss a new property development in your area. E-mails should be sent frequently but not so frequently that they become a nuisance. Again, the key is that each message should provide value to your customers or clients.

Blogs are informal communications between you, your customers, your employees, and anyone else who might be interested. They are opportunities to encourage word-of-mouth for your products, services, and brands and develop relationships with your customers on a personal level.

Blogs are usually less structured and "slick" than web sites. However, it is exactly those characteristics that make blogs credible, lead to their impact on your customers and potential customers, and help create "buzz." Your blog needs to be easy for others to find, engaging, up-to-date, and uninhibited. Let people know what is going on with you and let your personality shine through. Be careful your blog does not look like a sales pitch and be sure to include content that will make it worthwhile for people to stay in touch.

Calls   Warm calls come from referrals. You absolutely must respond to these as quickly as possible. The half-life of a warm call can be rather short. Have a package prepared—both digital and hard copy— that you can send to the referrals either before or after you talk to them. The package should contain information about you, your experience and abilities, and your clients—perhaps all that is covered in your brochure. I usually send general material before I contact the person. Then, after we have talked the first time, I send more detailed information that I think might meet their specific needs. In my case, the first set of materials is my brochure, the second set includes articles that I have written on the topics of concern to the prospective client.

Cold calls are a much different matter than warm calls. Cold calls may be unavoidable but you should try to be careful as to which ones you make. You need to set criteria about which cold calls you will pursue. These criteria might be based on the amount of business available or your estimate of your chances of winning the business. If you are making a cold call, try to warm it up by using your brochure in advance to build some interest before your initial contact.

Mass Communications   Mass communications includes all forms of advertising—direct mail, outdoor, newspaper, magazine, directory, radio, and television. At least at the beginning of building your personal brand, this type of communication will likely not be very cost-effective. The problem is that you will probably not be able to target customers as much as you would like. In addition, you may not be able to communicate your personal brand in the style that you'd like.

What you can do with mass communications is build awareness of your name. However, the other methods discussed will likely afford you more opportunity to develop associations between your personal attributes and your name.

Conclusion

You represent a brand and you need to manage your brand. Just like any branding situation, you need to focus on target customers and on those attributes you wish to connect to your personal brand. Then you need to live your brand in all the contacts you and your employees have with your customers. Be patient and committed and you will build a strong personal brand.

IV

BRANDING FOR REAL ESTATE

18

BRANDING REAL ESTATE
FOR THE SMALL INVESTOR

D oes branding work for the small real estate investor? Of course it
does.

Branding can help you raise the value of your property and it can
also help you sell it when you wish. As always, the key is to select a
brand position that is appealing to the customers in your target market. Then be consistent in communicating that position over time in
your actions and in your communications.

This chapter shows you how branding can be effective for the
small real estate investor.

THE SMALL REAL ESTATE INVESTOR

We are talking about the real estate investor with a single property,
most likely a garden apartment, low-rise apartment, or even middle-
rise apartment building. The single property might also be commercial
such as an office building or a community center or commercial lodging

such as a motel or motor hotel. Branding for real estate investors with more than one property is discussed in the next chapter.

If you are a small real estate investor, branding helps you in two ways:

1. Attracting and keeping tenants
2. Attracting and persuading buyers and lenders

The more tenants you have and the higher rents they pay you, the more your property is worth. Effective branding can affect the revenue and profits you receive from your tenants. In turn, your profits will have an impact on your ability to raise money and, should you decide to sell, your profits will have an impact on your selling price and even whether you find a purchaser.

Branding and Tenants

Your approach to branding tactics varies depending on whether you have a multiunit residential property, a commercial property, or an industrial property. For example, communications with potential residential customers will likely differ from those with potential commercial tenants. Your approach to branding strategy will, however, be the same.

Five steps for developing the tenant branding strategy:

1. Understand your tenants.
2. Select the tenants who are your target market.
3. Determine your brand position for your target tenants.
4. Improve the property as needed.
5. Communicate your brand position to your target tenants.

All of this information can be placed in a Real Estate Branding Plan (see Exhibit 18.1) that is similar to the plan discussed in Chapter 6 (Exhibit 6.2). The main difference is the addition of a section detailing plans for any needed property improvements.

Exhibit 18.1   Brand Plan for Real Estate*

Quarter	1	2	3	4
Financial Objectives				
Target Market and Positioning				
Property Improvements				
Branding Programs: Identifiers Advertising Promotion Public Relations Selling Internet				

Source: "Arrow Guide—Real Estate Branding," The Arrow Group, Ltd.®, New York, 2008. Used with permission. ***A blank version of this page can be downloaded from www.trumpuniversity .com/branding101 and customized for your personal use.*** For any other use, contact Don Sexton at Branding101@thearrowgroup.com.

Understand Your Tenants   The first and most basic rule in branding and marketing is: Know your customers. In this case, you need to know what your tenants want—aside from the lowest possible rent of course.

How do you find out what they want? The usual way—by talking with them. Note that asking someone for their opinion does not obligate you to agree with them or to take action based on their beliefs. If you are talking with your tenants, you should make clear in advance that you cannot solve all problems but want to know their concerns so you can keep them in mind and hopefully make changes that they will appreciate. Also be sure to emphasize that you are looking for things they like so you can keep doing them as well as things they don't like which you can improve.

Find out what your tenants like and don't like.

You might start by asking them a general question such as: "Why did you decide to rent here?" That question can lead to questions concerning any dissatisfactions they might have had with their prior location. Those answers can be very valuable in providing you with some knowledge of your competition.

Next you might ask general questions about the property such as: "What do you like about living (or doing business) here?" and "What would you like changed?"

You can follow up the general questions with more specific questions such as: "What do you think of the entry way," "the security arrangements," or "the custodial services?"

If your property has many tenants, you might consider asking these questions in a questionnaire. (Questionnaire design is discussed in the companion book, *Trump University Marketing 101*, Hoboken, NJ: Wiley, 2006.) However, even if you decide to use a questionnaire, you should first talk directly to some of your tenants because that will give you richer—more detailed—responses than are possible with a questionnaire.

Not only do you want to talk with your current tenants, you also want to talk with potential tenants. Suppose, for example, you have purchased a 12-unit apartment building near a university and you expect your tenants to be graduate students. You will find it valuable to chat with them about their problems in finding satisfactory housing. Then you can modify your property as necessary to meet their needs. Perhaps they would like a building with laundry facilities. You can decide if establishing a laundry room would be worthwhile for your investment.

From your discussions with tenants or possible tenants, you should have a list of their concerns and what they would like.

Select Your Target Tenant Market You may find that the needs of your tenants vary. The needs of seniors will likely differ from those of families with young children. Or, for a commercial property, the needs of an accounting firm will likely differ from those of a restaurant. You need to select those tenants on which you wish to focus your branding activities.

The second rule in branding and marketing is that you cannot be all things to all people. You need to concentrate your efforts (see Chapter 6).

You select your target tenants by considering how attractive they are to you as a group and how likely you are to attract them to your property.

Attractiveness consists of characteristics such as the rent you believe they might pay, their credit standing, and the costs of having them as a tenant. For example, I am on the board of a cooperative that rents our building's first floor (about 3000 square feet). When we have a vacancy, we give high priority to finding tenants such as architectural firms because they will not make great demands on the rather limited resources of our building.

Your relative ability to attract your target tenants depends on how well your property suits their needs and whether you can be effective in communicating the benefits of your property to them. If you own a retail center well-located in an affluent community, you may be able to attract clothing or other specialty stores that might appeal to those residents.

Note that when you select the tenants whom you do want, you are also selecting the tenants whom you do *not* want. Some prospective tenants may be those whom you want under no circumstances because they have a history of not paying rent or damaging property. Be sure you screen tenants—it is better to have no tenant than a bad tenant. Eviction can be costly and time consuming.

Determine Your Brand Position for Your Target Tenants Given your target market, you need to decide on a brand position. Your brand position should summarize for your target customer the reason that they should rent space in your property. Your brand position should be something your target customers want *and* something you can deliver.

Suppose you own an apartment building near a large corporation. You believe you can take advantage of the location to appeal to young married couples who work for that company. Your brand position might be convenience and your tag line something like "If you lived here, you'd be home by now."

Suppose you own a strip mall near a heavily used road. Your brand position might concern the amount of traffic a tenant might expect and your tag line, "Open your doors to more business."

Suppose you own a neighborhood center. Your brand position might be based on the ongoing relationship the center has with residents of the area and your tag line, "Sell where neighbors shop."

Your brand position should be something your target customers want and that you can deliver.

Improve the Property as Needed   Brands are promises to your target customers. Once-broken brand promises may not be believed again.

A terrific brand position well-communicated does not automatically lead to success. You also need to have a product or service that delivers or over-delivers what you promise. (That has long been the basis of the success of the Trump brand in real estate.)

Even if your apartment for young married couples is convenient, you still need to make sure that the units are appealing. Your apartment building for students may need to have a laundry room or a study room. Your strip center may require ample parking. Your neighborhood center may require more effort to keep the common areas clean.

A Trump saying is "Spend money where it can be seen." That means paying a bit more for the landscaping or for the entry lobby or the kitchen appliances. It will provide you a return. In particular, Donald Trump suggests that, "The right furniture, floor coverings, lighting all have a huge part to play in setting the stage for a property," and therefore—when you have the opportunity to make a change, consider it carefully (Jo Fleischer, "Household Name Donald Trump," *Home Furnishings Business*, March 26, 2007).

TRUMP TOWER AT CITY CENTER WHITE PLAINS

The 35-story Trump Tower at City Center in White Plains makes considerable use of granite and marble. The building has a black granite base and the floor of the landscaped plaza consists of a two-toned granite pattern. The interior lobby and penthouse corridor are finished with marble in the same striped pattern.

The kitchen countertops and backsplashes in all the condominium units are made of Kashmir White honed granite. Babu Reddy, president of Hindustan Granites, said that the blocks were chosen in India so that "the color range and property of the stone [would] be uniform throughout all the floors of the tower."

Source: Michelle Stinnard, "The Trump Tower at City Center in White Plains," *Stone World,* January, 2006, pp. 172–177.

Communicate Your Brand Position to Your Target Tenants You may know your brand position but until you tell your target customers, they won't know it.

You have many alternatives for communicating with your target customers but clearly you want to find ways that are cost effective. Options include the following:

- Identifiers—name, tag line, logo
- Signs and billboards
- Business cards, brochures, flyers
- Events
- Public relations
- Web site, e-mail, blogs
- Direct mail
- Calls on customers or potential customers
- Mass communications

You can develop a focus for the brand identity of your property by choosing a name or tag line, even a logo. This may seem like overkill for a single property but if you acquire more properties, you may be able to use the brand name for all your properties. If you specialize in housing for seniors, perhaps your brand name might be Platinum Age Housing and your tag line "Live your golden years in platinum style." (You can no doubt do better.)

If you have a brand name, tag line, or logo, it should be prominently featured on *all* your materials. Your signs—directional or informational—all should include your brand identifiers. Be somewhat careful of where you place "For Rent" signs because they sometimes invite vandalism. If possible, leave window treatments up so a unit does not appear unoccupied.

Billboards should include not only your brand name but also the key attribute of your brand position. Choose billboard locations where your target tenants are most likely to see them. Suppose you have a small motel on the Las Vegas strip situated among enormous competitors. You might use humor to make your business stand out:

Las Vegas motel and sign.
Photo credit: Don Sexton. Photos courtesy of Don Sexton.

Your business cards should function as tiny billboards for your property. You should certainly prepare flyers and, if it is cost-effective for you, brochures. When preparing flyers and brochures, give a lot of space to the attribute that is your brand position. You can list all the other wonderful attributes you provide to your tenants but do not make it appear that all attributes are equal. Otherwise your materials will seem like the old automobile ads where having a light in the glove compartment seemed to be as important as safety or fuel efficiency. Your brand attributes were chosen because they are important to your target customer and because you do them well—so flaunt them.

Events include open houses. Plan the event so it runs smoothly and you have time to talk with prospective tenants and answer their questions. Have plenty of flyers or brochures available and be sure to capture the contact information of anyone who attends.

If there is a way to make your event newsworthy, do it. For example, you might have a local musician perform or a local financial advisor provide a talk. Public relations can work efficiently and effectively but you need a story line to catch the eye of the local editor. If you are making major modifications in your property or reopening a property that has been dormant, these may be story lines. To get them to the attention of editors, you need to describe them in a press release. Contact your local newspaper, magazine, radio station, or television station to learn what format they prefer for a press release.

Make your events newsworthy.

If your target audience is often online, you should consider having a web site for the property. For example, if you are trying to attract college students or young singles, a web site may be very effective for you. The site need not be elaborate but obviously it should present your brand position, give information about the units (perhaps photos), and your contact information. You can also send e-mails describing any improvements made to your property or set up a blog to provide ongoing information as to what you are doing to make the property attractive to tenants.

If you have a commercial property, you may already have identified prospective tenants. For tenants that are economically attractive, it may be worthwhile for you to make personal calls. If the prospective tenant already knows you, then you would be making a *warm call* which is far preferable to making a *cold call*. However, you can warm cold calls up a bit before your visit by sending prospects a letter with your flyer or brochure. You can also e-mail them similar information with a link to your web site. Calls should be planned in advance—not scripted— because you want to listen to the concerns of your prospective client. Planned means you have an overall strategy for the call—the points you will make and what you hope to achieve by the call—Gain interest? Invite for a visit of the property? Sign a lease?

Mass communications covers all forms of advertising from a classified ad in the newspaper, to direct mail, to larger scale ads in the print and broadcast media. It is difficult to say in general what might be right for you because single properties can vary considerably in size and in income-generating potential. Most mass media ads will *not* close the deal. You will still need to employ some other means of communication such as a brochure, a visit to your web site, or a sales call on site to provide potential tenants with sufficient information for them to make their decision.

However, there are some economical media buys for the small real estate investor. For example, local cable often groups ads for real estate and may be a relatively inexpensive way to make your brand known.

Overall, when communicating with your target customers, use as many different means as are economically feasible and keep them all consistent with respect to your brand position.

Maintaining Your Brand with Tenants

Once you have tenants, continue to maintain your brand.

You may want to recognize their move-in day with a small touch such as a bouquet of flowers in their living room.

During their tenancy, be clear about what you are responsible for and follow through when they make reasonable requests. Answer their telephone calls and e-mails promptly. After high rent, lack of follow-through on maintenance is probably the largest reason for tenant dissatisfaction. As Paul Heal of Laing Homes in the United Kingdom cautions, "Buyers are pretty fair-minded about snagging problems, they realize that certain things are outside the control of a developer. What they can't stand is being told someone will be there to fix it on Thursday and then no one turning up" (David Spittles, "Building Brand Loyalty," *Evening Standard*, March 31, 2004, pp. 6–7).

Remember you and your employees *are* the brand to your tenants.

BRANDING AND BUYERS AND LENDERS

If you are selling a property just once, then it may not make sense to brand only for the purpose of influencing that single buyer. You still may want to brand your apartment building or strip mall to influence tenants. However, if you are regularly buying and selling properties, then it can help to have a brand that is known. Brands make the buying process simpler for the purchaser by providing information about you. If you are known and have a sound reputation for selling properties of a certain type, that can help you with brokers and with the buyers themselves. A strong brand can also help persuade lenders to provide you money.

The steps for developing a buyer branding strategy are very similar to the steps for developing the tenant branding strategy:

1. Understand your potential buyers.
2. Select the potential buyers who are your target market.
3. Determine your brand position for your target buyers.
4. Improve the property as needed.
5. Communicate your brand position to your target buyers.

STUDYING THE TRUMP REAL ESTATE BRAND

In a recent study of the Trump brand, conducted by Millward Brown Optimor and sponsored by Nakheel, among people interested in purchasing luxury property in Dubai, 86 percent of the

---

(continued)

respondents agreed with the statement that "The Trump brand means luxury" and 78 percent agreed that "The Trump brand is a truly premium brand."

Brokers who were contacted during the survey described the Trump brand:

"Trump is luxury, excellence, elegance, glamour, services, sophistication, and prestige."

"Trump is excitement."

"What people rave about is the level of services and the people who are delivering those services."

"I have always wanted to own in a Trump building in terms of the whole ownership experience."

Overall, the Trump brand was found to have "no perceived drawbacks."

More than 50 percent of those surveyed said that there is a higher chance of their buying a condominium in Trump Tower in Dubai versus any other luxury condominium. Of those respondents, 53 percent expected to pay a price premium of 20 percent and an additional 34 percent expected to pay a price premium of 33 percent or more.

_____

Source: Millward Brown Optimor, "Trump Brand Study," 2008.

Understand Your Potential Buyers

Your reasons for buying the property—perhaps return on investment—may be the same as those of your prospective buyers but do not assume that. They may have different expectations than you as regards amount of return, timing of return, and amount of involvement with the property. The only way to find out what a potential buyer wants is to ask.

If you are selling your property just this once, it may not be worthwhile to go through the trouble of building a brand. However, if you expect to make a series of sales, you may wish to develop a brand for your company (or yourself—see Chapter 17).

Select Your Target Buyer Market   Once you know the expectations of all of your potential buyers, you need to decide which ones are most attractive to you and which ones you believe will want the type of property you have. For example, if you have a mid-rise rental apartment property that provides a steady income, that will appeal to some buyers while a low-rise fixer-upper apartment property might appeal to others.

Determine Your Brand Position for Your Target Buyers   Your brand position for your tenants should provide a foundation for your brand position for buyers. That is, if you are selling units to young married couples on the basis of convenient location, that brand position should support whatever financial appeals you are presenting to your target buyers for the overall property. What your target buyers are purchasing from you is a cash flow. Your tenant brand position is part of the reason for that cash flow.

Your brand position for tenants is the foundation for your brand position for buyers.

Improve the Property as Needed   Buyers may not want to deal with some issues to your property in its present state. You may need to repair or replace or clean before the deal can be made. Again, keep in mind the maxim, spend generously where the money can be seen.

Communicate Your Brand Position to Your Target Buyers   Buyers for your property will likely be less numerous than possible tenants. That means your brand communications for buyers should be more targeted than your brand communications for tenants. Communications approaches should include well-designed and well-produced brochures, warm and cold calls, and personal direct mail (personalized letters). The emphasis should be on tailored communications whenever possible.

Conclusion

Branding can work to increase demand or prices or both for any product or service, including real estate property. The small real estate investor can enhance their returns by paying attention to their brand. Brand-building need not cost a lot, but it does require communicating with potential customers, determining a brand position, and using the brand position to guide actions and communications.

(For more on managing real estate, see *Trump University Real Estate 101*, Hoboken, NJ: Wiley, 2006.)

19

BRANDING REAL ESTATE FOR THE LARGE INVESTOR

One afternoon I spent an hour browsing through the real estate section of a large well-known bookstore in Manhattan. Some of the real estate books had "marketing" in their index but none had "branding" in their index. I even reviewed their marketing pages and found no mention of branding in those paragraphs.

Branding *is* important to the real estate investor. Branding helps you charge premium prices or rent or sell more units or—very often—both. The lack of branding advice in most real estate books is unfortunate. This chapter tries to close that gap by showing you how branding can significantly improve your real estate investments.

THE LARGE REAL ESTATE INVESTOR

This chapter is for the large real estate investor who typically owns multiple properties—apartments, office buildings, retailing centers, hotels, industrial buildings. Or you may own a single large property such as a mixed-use site. Branding helps the large real estate investor in four primary ways:

1. Attracting and keeping tenants.
2. Attracting and persuading buyers and lenders.
3. Attracting and keeping potential employees.
4. Influencing public and government opinion.

The first two uses of branding are similar to those we discussed for the small investor in Chapter 18. For the large investor, however, there are two other uses for branding. A well-known, reputable brand can help you recruit employees who want to be part of your operation. The brand can also help you retain those employees. Human resources managers always benefit from a strong brand.

The remaining use—influencing the public—is important to the large real estate investor precisely because they have large projects that will be in the public eye and in the media. A well-established reputation can reassure the public that a project will make a positive contribution to the community.

BRANDING AND TENANTS

For a large real estate investor, branding can have significant leverage on your profits and cash flow because your brand can affect the occupancy of all your properties. Aircraft are not worth anything to airlines if they are without passengers. Buildings are worth much less to you (or to prospective buyers of your property) if they are without occupants.

Your brand can help you attract the tenants you prefer and also help you keep them. When I was working on a marketing project for The Mart—a collection of shops in midtown New York City, we carefully tracked the number of people entering the shopping complex by specific entrances so we could better understand which stores or what types of stores were attracting the traffic. That helped us determine what stores were needed to assure continuous demand.

Any vacancy is a lost opportunity for revenue and profits, never to return. Often investors wait to market a vacancy when it becomes apparent that there will be a vacancy and that means a possible lag in securing a new tenant. In contrast, branding provides you with what is in effect *continuous marketing* so that when there is a vacancy, there will likely be less time before a new tenant moves in.

Branding provides you with continuous marketing.

In real estate, rents depend on a variety of factors—many relating to the features of the property such as curb appeal or parking availability. If you have a brand, your brand can impact the rents your tenants will pay. Note that the impact should be positive but it can be negative if you are not careful and do not monitor your brand.

In New York City, for example, many buildings that are on Park Avenue but have their entry-way on a side street invariably use Park Avenue as their address. Why? Because Park Avenue itself is a brand with attributes that tenants enjoy and enjoy communicating to others.

You can do the same with your property brand whether it is for residential or commercial property.

Five steps for developing the tenant branding strategy:

1. Understand your tenants.
2. Select the tenants who are your target market.
3. Determine your brand position for your target tenants.
4. Improve the property as needed.
5. Communicate your brand position to your target tenants.

Your Real Estate Branding Plan is similar to that discussed in the preceding chapter (Exhibit 18.1). The difference is that now the plan needs to cover many more properties and you may need a separate planning page for each property.

Understand Your Tenants   You begin any branding or marketing strategy by finding out as much as you can about your tenants.

A large investor might consider surveying potential tenants. However, before any survey is conducted, you will find it useful to gather information more informally. You or someone you employ should talk to possible tenants. If you already have some idea of the type of tenants in which you are interested, you might focus your attention on them. If at the outset you do not know who your customers are, you should approach the market broadly and deliberately try to contact a variety of possible tenants.

Initial contacts may be in-person or by telephone but should be relatively unstructured. You want to hear what these tenants think about existing properties, what they like or don't like, and what would attract them to your property. For example, perhaps an architectural firm requires an expansive, well-lit space while a realty firm requires numerous communications connections. After digesting these replies, you might consider a more formal method of acquiring customer information such as a survey. (Constructing a questionnaire is discussed in the companion book, *Trump University Marketing 101*, Hoboken, NJ: Wiley, 2006.)

What you need to learn are the benefits that different types of possible tenants consider as high priorities. If you are going to persuade them to become your tenants, then you need to be able to provide those benefits *better* than your competitors.

You also should consider learning about the habits and preferences of your tenants' potential customers because their behavior will often determine the attractiveness of your property to your potential tenants. You can both ask about their behavior and watch them.

I was responsible for a large survey of users of Central Park. This was not a study of a real estate property but was similar in that we were trying to obtain opinions about a space people visited much as they might visit a mall. We watched what people did in the park and also conducted numerous in-person and telephone interviews. We were able to estimate the number of visitors to Central Park, discover what they liked to do, and found that what most people wanted in the park was more "cops and flowers." (The results of the study were used to justify a larger budget for the park operations.) A similar approach—combining interviews and observations—can be used to study the visitors at any commercial site.

Select Your Target Tenant Market Attractiveness is one of the two main dimensions you use to select target tenant markets. You need to develop a profile of the type of tenant you want. The attractiveness of a potential tenant will most certainly include their level of financial responsibility and their ability to pay rents that will allow your property to be profitable. You will also want to consider how long you might expect them to remain and how that might affect your financial return. If the prospective tenant is a business, then you want to evaluate whether you believe that business will succeed.

Note that for some types of property certain tenants are attractive because they will attract other tenants. For example, Saks Fifth Avenue was invited to Japan by commercial facility developers to operate 5 to 10 stores in Tokyo. These stores are located in spaces in the properties that would be too small for traditional Japanese department stores that have much broader product lines than the fashion-specialist Saks Fifth Avenue. The presence of Saks, in turn, might attract other tenants ("Commercial Developers Behind Saks Entering Japan," *Nikkei Weekly* [Japan], September 22, 2003). Similarly, the retailers in the Bal Harbour Shops in Florida attract other retailers with the same appeal.

Other concerns might include your evaluation of their respect for property and the condition in which you expect them to leave your property when they move on.

Your relative ability to satisfy your tenants is the second dimension you use to select target tenant markets. Relative ability to satisfy tenants depends on how your capabilities, including the features of your property, match up with what the potential tenants are looking for. For example, access to transportation for a warehousing/distribution center or proximity to hospitals for medical offices. Convenience to shopping for seniors or willingness to provide short-term leases for students.

Bal Harbour Shops advertisement.

Ideally your target market should consist of tenants that are attractive to you and whom you believe you can attract to your property.

Determine Your Brand Position for Your Target Tenants   When you are considering your choice of target market, you should also be considering your brand position. As you know from prior chapters, your brand position should consist of one or two (at most three) of the benefits sought by your target tenants.

Having the relative ability to attract tenants is one of the reasons you selected your target group of tenants. Your relative ability to attract tenants should be directly translatable into your brand position. If you have a regional shopping center with a beautiful atrium, a supervised play space for young children, and a collection of unique vendors in your food court, then your brand position for prospective tenants might be based on how the pleasant experience of shopping at your center will draw buyers. If you target fashion-forward retailers as shops for your center, then your brand position might be based on how being a style and fashion center will attract customers. If your regional shopping center is located near major thoroughfares and has ample parking space, then your brand position for your tenants might focus on the ease with which shoppers can get to your center.

Your brand position is the theme for your branding strategy. That is why you should not try to include too many benefits in the position. Your target tenants will not remember all of the benefits and they will have no clear mental picture as to why your property is unique. The power of a brand is to simplify decisions for customers—not to complicate them.

I was asked to help businesses in St. Lucia with their positioning—not an easy problem. There are a number of islands in the Caribbean and all of them can develop brand positioning on sun and sea. However, if everyone does that, then no one will be unique.

In my advertising class, I give my students the problem of developing a brand position for a Greek island. I divide the class into teams and assign each of them a different island such as Mykonos or Paros or Crete. Each team then prepares a presentation—a "pitch"—as if they were an advertising agency seeking the tourism advertising campaign for the island assigned to them. I invite a creative director from an advertising agency to listen to and comment on their presentations. The creative directors always make the same observations, namely, that most of the presentations are interchangeable because they focus on the same position of sun and sea. The presentations that stand out are the ones where the team has been able to find some characteristic of their island that is distinctive *and* that would be appealing to a target segment.

Improve the Property as Needed   You must keep your brand promise otherwise it may wear out quickly. That means you need to be sure that your property delivers whatever your brand position offers.

If your regional center promises a pleasant shopping experience, then you must do whatever is needed to make that so. The atrium, child play area, and food court must all be as you claim.

As mentioned in Chapter 18, a key Trump real estate principle is, "Spend money where it will be seen." In a regional shopping center, that means spending money on the ambience—even if you feel you are overpaying. It is difficult to evaluate the return on expenditures on features such as an atrium—you need to trust that they will be reflected in your brand and how it is regarded by prospective customers.

Certainly you need to spend money as needed to maintain your property whether the improvement is visible or not. However, if there are two alternatives of equal effectiveness, then you would choose the less expensive method if the appearance aesthetics would not have any impact on the brand or the success of the property.

PENTHOUSE SUITES AT TRUMP TAJ MAHAL

The Penthouse Suites at the Trump Taj Mahal were designed to provide luxury accommodations for their most exclusive guests. Designed by Wilson and Associates, each suite is inspired by the interiors of palaces and grand hotels in Europe.

The largest suite, The Alexander, "offers a sprawling 4,000 square feet of opulence." It includes a grand parlor with a baby grand piano. The table in the dining room is crafted from exotic woods and the place settings are from Bernardaud and Christolfe. There are designer touches throughout such as the luxury bedding by Chaz Stevens of Beverly Hills. From anywhere in the suite, you have panoramic views of the ocean and Atlantic City.

All the penthouse suites have received the same Trump attention to detail—imported marble, custom-made furnishings, hand-tufted wool carpets, steam showers, and state-of-the-art audio and video systems. Art works from specially selected regional artists were commissioned for the suites and include contemporary and traditional paintings, drawings, and sculptures.

According to the head designer for the project, Michael Medeiros, "Our inspiration was the challenge of creating a complete luxury experience from the moment you enter the 51st

---

Interior of Alexander Suite, Trump Taj Mahal, Atlantic City.
Photo credit: Michael Spain Smith. Photo courtesy of the Trump Organization.

floor. We wanted to provide the guest a tranquil respite from the otherwise stimulating excitement of the casino floor."

Source: "The Penthouse Suites at Trump Taj Mahal Offer the Ultimate Extravagant Hotel Experience," Trump Taj Mahal press release, October 11, 2007.

Communicate Your Brand Position to Your Target Tenants

Although you know what you are providing your tenants and you know your brand position, you cannot assume that the tenants know your brand position. For your brand position to be effective, you must tell your target customers what your brand position is, repeatedly and consistently over time. You have many communication vehicles from which to choose. You should likely use multiple vehicles, being careful that they all are in agreement all the time.

Use multiple communications.

Communication vehicles include:

- Identifiers—name, tag line, logo
- Signs and billboards
- Business cards and stationery
- Brochures
- Events
- Public relations
- Internet
- Direct mail
- Telemarketing
- In-person calls on customers or potential customers
- Print media
- Broadcast media
- Sales office and model units

Select your brand name with some care. A brand name should immediately cue the target tenant about the attributes of your brand position. Your logo should be dramatic and support your brand position. Feature your brand name and logo in all communications concerning your properties. If each of your properties has a different name or logo, you will not benefit from your overall branding effort.

When you hear Mandarin Hotels, what kind of hotels come to mind? Superb service. Luxury accommodations. As recounted in Chapter 3, for a long while, every hotel in the Mandarin chain was going its own way with its brand communications. The Mandarin Hong Kong brand would be different from the Mandarin Jakarta brand which would be different from the Mandarin Bangkok brand. Doing nothing else but changing and unifying the logo—an oriental fan—with no increase in media spending, Mandarin hotels saw their occupancy rate go up about 40 percent in just one year. This impact occurred because the use of the common logo enabled the individual hotels to reinforce the same brand position to business travelers.

Mandarin management allowed their hotels to advertise locally for guests and for other local business such as wedding planners. This local advertising had the same general look across the hotels and employed the oriental fan logo. Each hotel emphasized different services to their local markets. The impact of the local branding campaigns—with the unifying logo—was to increase each hotel's yield (room rate times occupancy) more than 30 percent within a year.

Even in an Internet world, a substantial brochure can be very effective. Do not scrimp on the production values of your brochure. Your brochure is your brand and should communicate your brand position with verve and drama.

Try to attract prospective tenants by scheduling events at your properties. They may be charity events or seminars but you hope they will draw people to see the inside of your property. Curb appeal—what people see on the outside—is important but to solidify your brand image, you must persuade them to come inside.

Public relations requires events that editors consider newsworthy. With established properties, you may be able to schedule events such as a holiday concert in your atrium. If you are in the process of building

Mandarin Oriental Hotel advertisements.

the property, there are many newsworthy events such as the signing of key contracts, the groundbreaking, and the topping-off.

Where I grew up near Hartford, Connecticut, there was a famous drive-in movie theater that many baby boomers remembered with fondness. Recently, it was torn down to make way for a new housing development. Photos of the razing of the giant movie screen appeared in all the local media and was effective publicity for the developer.

Many tenants search online for commercial or residential space. You certainly need to have a web site that includes photos, key information, and how to reach you. Direct mail enables you to focus on target groups of tenants. You can also employ telemarketing. However, if you do, make sure that those making the calls have the key talking points or even a script that will help them support your brand position.

If you have a large property such as a mixed-use complex, it may well be worthwhile for you to utilize personal selling techniques. Any sales contact needs to be orchestrated to build on the foundation of your brand position.

Hartford Drive-In shortly before razing.
Photo credit: Don Sexton. Photo courtesy of Don Sexton.

Print media include newspapers and magazines. Whether these media will work for you depends on how many possible potential tenants are in your target market. For example, if your properties are high-rise residential then print media become more efficient and effective. If your property is a regional center where you already have an idea of the retailers you wish to entice, then print media may not be very efficient but targeted personal selling would be. The same comments are true for other mass media such as radio and television.

Your sales office and your model units also are part of your brand communications. Your sales office should of course be easy to find and convenient. Your staff should understand your brand and communicate your brand position. (See Chapter 23 for more discussion concerning employees and your brand.)

Commercial model units should display all the features and services that are available. Residential model units should be decorated with furniture and art to appeal to the tastes of the members of your target market. Be careful that the furniture is not too large or too plentiful—that makes the unit appear small. Remember all the senses—maybe have bread or cookies baking in the oven.

TRUMP ENTERTAINMENT RESORTS NEW YEAR'S EVE

Trump Entertainment Resorts uses a variety of approaches to keep current customers and attract new customers.

For New Year's Eve, you typically have your choice of a wide variety of parties and packages, such as:

New Year's Eve Overnight Package—one night accommodation, admission to a themed party, dinner, and brunch.

Regatta Room Package—dinner and admission to party.

The Wave Package—admission to party.

Gourmet Dinner and Wave Package—dinner and admission to party.

(continued)

New Year's Eve Party at Trump Taj Mahal, Atlantic City
Photo credit: Dominic Episcopo. Photo courtesy of the Trump Taj Mahal.

Gourmet Dinner and Shell Package—dinner and admission to show.

New Year's Eve at The Casbah.

New Year's Eve '70s Dance Party.

Each package or party is specifically targeted to a different group of customers and a different price level.

Source: "Ring in the New Year with Parties, Overnight Packages at Trump Entertainment Resorts," Trump Entertainment Resort press release, December 27, 2007.

BRANDING AND BUYERS AND LENDERS

If you have developed a strong brand for tenant markets, then that brand should work for prospective buyers of your property or prospective lenders should you need to raise money for improvements or additions.

Your brand for tenants will allow you to have high occupancy at above-market prices and that should be persuasive to possible buyers of your property or possible lenders.

To develop the buyer branding strategy, you need to follow steps similar to those for developing the tenant branding strategy:

1. Understand your potential buyers.
2. Select the potential buyers who are your target market.
3. Determine your brand position for your target buyers.
4. Improve the property as needed.
5. Communicate your brand position to your target buyers.

Understand Your Potential Buyers Potential buyers may differ as regards the type of financial return they expect and when they expect it. You can use your tenant branding position to support your revenue, profit, and cash flow estimates.

Select Your Target Buyer Market The expected financial performance of your property may meet the objectives of some potential buyers better than others. You should concentrate your branding efforts on those potential buyers that are attractive to you and to whom you believe your property will be of interest.

Determine Your Brand Position for Your Target Buyers Most likely you will use your tenant brand position as the basis for your brand position with your target buyers. You need to emphasize the relationship of that brand position to the financial value of your property.

Improve the Property as Needed If your property needs to be improved to continue your brand promise to your tenants, that must be made clear in your dealings with potential buyers. You may need to make those improvements before the deal is closed.

Communicate Your Brand Position to Your Target Buyers The brand communications methods you will use for potential buyers will probably be much more focused than you use for tenants simply because the target market of buyers for your property numbers relatively few customers compared to the target markets for your tenants. For example, sales calls will likely be much more important in building your brand directly with buyers. On the other hand, all your communications efforts to build your brand for tenants should also affect your potential buyers.

Brand communications for potential buyers will be more focused than for potential tenants.

CONCLUSION

Branding can appreciably raise your rents and increase your occupancy rates. For new properties, branding can increase the rate at which new tenants sign up.

For a successful real estate brand, you must find attributes that are important to tenants and buyers, then deliver them and communicate them. As Donald Trump has stated, "A lot of people who don't know me think that I'm a great promoter but the fact is what I do the best is build so I build a great product and then it sells and everyone gives me credit for being a good promoter. . . . I build really high quality buildings. I think I do well in promotion because I build a great product."

Great products are the key to all branding, including the branding of real estate.

(For more on managing real estate, see *Trump University Real Estate 101*, Hoboken, NJ: Wiley, 2006.)

20

MANAGING YOUR REAL
ESTATE BRAND

Branded properties provide you with higher prices and higher demand. The brand also is a growth platform for your future projects.

If you are a developer, branding real estate should not be viewed just on a project-by-project basis. Branding is a long-term strategic decision. To achieve success with brands, they must be managed carefully and consistently over time.

This chapter explains how to build your real estate brand and keep it powerful.

DONALD J. TRUMP ON REAL ESTATE BRANDING

"I see a lot of people who do things wrong in marketing. I know one developer who can never understand why I get so much more per square foot than he does. He just finished this building

(continued)

where he's got these tiny little windows and terrible color brick. It's just an unattractive building. And then I blow him away and he goes around telling people he doesn't understand why Trump gets higher prices than he does. The guy doesn't have a clue. The mistakes in marketing often have to do with mistakes in the product.

"Branding is an important part of marketing. The Trump brand stands for very high quality and very high confidence. People feel secure in the brand. That's why my building in Las Vegas is so successful. Other builders are not doing well and I'm doing very well. Because of the Trump brand, people buy in my buildings without ever having seen the units. They don't do that with other builders. My customers know the building's going to be the highest quality, the best architecture, and the best location."

Impact of the Real Estate Brand

Developers acquire the rights to a property and prepare it for a different use—residential, commercial, or mixed-use. Investors—unless they are developers as well—do not usually participate in the process of substantially altering the property, developers are active in that process, which includes building the real estate brand.

Branding should simplify the purchasing process for the customer. The impact of any brand depends on the significance of the purchase and the concerns of the target customer and their ability to pay. You expect a brand to have relatively more impact the more sensitive the customer is to reputation and the more able the customer is to pay for their needs. That means the real estate brand likely has the most impact on properties at the high end of the market where brand intangibles related to luxury and credibility are more important. The managing director of one British property marketing company observed that you can charge for "an extra point of difference," but only if the brand provides a feeling "of confidence, superiority, and comfort"

(Catherine J. Moye, "Glamour by Association," *Financial Times*, October 25, 2003, p. 12).

Branding should simplify the purchasing process for the customer.

During quiet times, tenants or buyers may be less sensitive to a real estate brand. However, during noisy times such as recessions, tenants and buyers may be quite concerned about the reputation—the brand—of a developer. The brand can reassure the customer before they choose to sign a contract. A senior vice president in one development company concluded that, "During the recession . . . , when there were many cases of developers who were unable to complete their projects after taking money from buyers, home seekers began to realize the importance of a developer's track record and reputation" ("Developers Sell on Brand, Site, and Price," *Star*, September 23, 2003, p. 1).

While a brand can provide differentiation for your property, it cannot offset poor construction. As Donald Trump has often stated, "You need a great product—one that your customers want and will pay for." Mar-a-Lago is the former mansion of Marjorie Merriwether Post in Palm Beach, Florida, which was transformed by Donald Trump into a luxurious country club. All the material utilized in the restoration, such as stonework and marble, were the highest grade. The staff of Mar-a-Lago includes a world-class chef and headline entertainers are brought in on weekends. A great product is the foundation for a great brand.

A brand cannot compensate for a poor product.

All real estate people know that location matters too. According to one real estate consultant. "If the location's not good, you can call it

Mar-a-Lago.
Photo credit: Don Sexton. Photo courtesy of Don Sexton.

Armani, but it ain't going to help" (Lucy Denyer, "All the Right Labels," *Sunday Times*, January 7, 2007, p. 4).

DEVELOPMENT BRANDING PLAN

The business plan for a real estate project includes the marketing plan that in turn includes the branding plan. A typical branding plan includes an evaluation of the size of the potential market, the demand objectives for the project, the brand positioning, and the communications that will be required.

The components of the branding plan are like those described in Chapter 18 (Exhibit 18.1), but on a larger scale. The six steps to prepare the real estate branding plan are similar to those discussed in Chapters 18 and 19:

1. Evaluate the real estate environment.
2. Understand your tenants.
3. Select the tenants who are your target market.
4. Determine your brand position for your target tenants.

5. Design and alter the property as needed.
6. Communicate your brand position to your target tenants.

One major difference between this plan and those described in Chapters 18 and 19 is the need to do a more comprehensive situation analysis—an evaluation of all the dimensions of the real estate environment. The other major difference in the contents of the plan is that the changes made in the property will usually be much more significant than those discussed for existing properties in the prior chapters.

Evaluate the Real Estate Environment   A developer needs to understand the directions of growth in an area and anticipate their effects on the demand for real estate. According to Donald Trump, a key to developing is "having the vision to see where the world is going to be, so when the building is completed they are standing in line to get in" (Steven Bergsman, *Maverick Real Estate Investing*, Hoboken, NJ: Wiley, 2004, p. 12).

For example, if the number of married couples with children is declining while the number of single-parent households is increasing, those trends have important implications for the types of residential properties that need to be developed. More generally, the developer needs to have a broad view and comprehend changes not only in demographics but in technology, politics, regulations, culture, and the economy. (See Chapter 8 of *Trump University Marketing 101*, Hoboken, NJ: Wiley, 2006, for a full discussion of how to do a situation analysis.)

To obtain that broad view, the developer should stay in touch with many sources of information such as Internet reports, e-zines, newspapers, and industry publications. The more sources they subscribe to or check, the more the chances they will spot a trend, such as revitalization signs for a neighborhood, that will provide the basis for a possible project.

Stay in touch with multiple sources of information.

Understand Your Tenants   As always, sound branding and marketing strategies are based on knowledge of your customers. Many developers rely on their observations of customers and their discussions with customers for their market knowledge. However, you may also want to conduct a survey—perhaps on an ongoing basis.

A survey should include questions concerned with requirements for space and location as well as specific questions regarding preferences for building features such as layout, parking, security, and utilities. The survey responses differ depending on whether the properties are intended for residential, commercial, or mixed-use. For example, residential units require different amounts and different kinds of parking than a strip mall.

Select Your Target Tenant Market   Your marketing research serves as the basis for choosing your target market. In Montreal, Prevel Group used focus groups and surveys to help them with their branding decisions for the launch of their Leloft condominiums. They targeted young, first-time owners who would likely want a small, stylish apartment in a trendy area. Their marketing materials featured a young couple riding an old two-seater bicycle and the colors of their logo were similar to those on the box of Cherry Blossoms chocolate that used to be made in a factory on the site (Mary Lamey, "Marketing a Lifestyle," *Gazette*, November 13, 2004, p. E1).

Determine Your Brand Position for Your Target Tenants   Brands allow you to build distinction in your customer's mind. There are a variety of possible positions for the real estate brand.

Some developers have adopted a "green" position—that their buildings more efficiently utilize the resources of society such as water, energy, and land. For example, South Group has received an award from the U.S. Green Building Council for their Elleven Tower in Los Angeles, which has bamboo floors, energy-efficient temperature systems, and windows that open (allowing more savings on air-conditioning (Roger Vincent, "So What's Up in Downtown LA?" *Los Angeles Times*, November 13, 2007, p. C-1).

Well-known architects can provide distinction to a project. Peter Slatin, publisher of *The Slatin Report,* a New York–based real estate newsletter, points out that "Name-brand architecture sells better than your typical vanilla box" These architects create exacting designs that appeal to the high-end buyer ("Big Apple Residential Developers Embracing 'Signature' Architects," *Architectural Record,* June 1, 2005, p. 28). Adds Christine DeGasperis, marketing manager for Aspen Ridge, "You almost have to hire a dream team now. Architects are becoming minor celebrities. We are pushing the names from a marketing standpoint to garner attention to the project" (Diane Tierney, "What's in a Name?" *Toronto Star,* June 2, 2007, p. CO 01).

DESIGN

The designs of the Trump Hotel Collection properties are often quite distinctive and enhance the brand.

Trump Hotel Collection, Dubai and Panama
Photos courtesy of the Trump Organization.

To distinguish their offerings, some developers are adding art— paintings and sculptures—to their properties. In the United Kingdom, for example, St. James Homes Group has set up an Arts Foundation that guides the placement of art in their properties and has ties to galleries. James Davies, a development consultant, notes St. James' art policy ". . . gives the impression that St. James is a developer that cares about what they are building" (Clare Dowdy, "Home Is Where the Art Is," *Financial Times*, December 13, 2003, p. 15).

Others have taken an approach based on fashion, even hiring designers to design details for their lobbies. Peter Som, a fashion designer, was hired by one developer to work with the architects. He designed the lobby staircase and selected the fabric for the chairs in the lobby lounge. One tenant said the fashion connection appealed to him because it would draw to the building "people with certain qualities I like. People a little bit on the edge that love fashion and the excitement that fashion creates" (Ruth La Perla, "Nests Imperial or Fashionably Feathered," *New York Times*, February 2, 2006, p. 1). Armani is working with Emaar Properties to develop ten hotels and four resorts throughout the world ("Stretch Your Brand," *Business & Finance*, February 24, 2005). Ritz-Carlton has partnered with Bulgari for hotels in Milan and in Bali. Versace offers interior-design services for resorts and offices and provides Versace-designed furniture, linens, and lamps for the Palazzo Versace on Australia's Gold Coast (Lim Lay Ying, "Taking the Brand Approach," *New Straits Times*, February 3, 2007, p. 10).

Marriott International hired Ian Schrager, famous as the co-founder of New York's Studio 54 nightclub and an ultra-hip icon, to design about 100 boutique hotels (Ron Stodghill, "Going Boutique on a Large Scale," *International Herald Tribune*, August 22, 2007, p. 8). This appears to be part of their strategy to reposition the Marriott brand. "We want to go from being a logical choice to a brand that's loved," stated Michael E. Jannini, Marriott's chief brand manager (Catherine Yang and Diane Brady, "Marriott Hip? Well, It's Trying," *BusinessWeek*, September 26, 2005, p. 70).

Design and Alter the Property as Needed   The design of the property will be consistent with your market understanding and your brand position. Marriott is transforming some of its Courtyard lobbies into "great rooms" because they have found some guests "prefer inviting public spaces for working to holing up in their rooms" (Catherine Yang and Diane Brady, "Marriott Hip? Well, It's Trying," *Business-Week*, September 26, 2005, p. 70).

A shopping center is often a traditional mall with anchor stores and specialty shops or it may be a "big box campus." Recently, there has been a trend to malls that are lifestyle centers. Typically, in a lifestyle center the stores are arranged in rows or a square around a parking lot. The architecture of the buildings varies but are designed to be attractive, giving the effect of a small village where shoppers might mingle. There are no anchor stores similar to those in traditional malls and no big-box stores. Instead, there are upscale stores such as Whole Foods and Williams-Sonoma. The objective is to create an ambience where customers will come to enjoy shopping (Emily Shartin, "Goodbye Mall, Hello Lifestyle Center," *Boston Globe*, August 21, 2005, p. 4).

According to a study by the International Council of Shopping Centers, the average length of stay of a customer at a lifestyle center was about 27 percent shorter than at a traditional mall but more intensively used, 51 percent more sales per hour. Three-quarters of those surveyed said that they visited the lifestyle center because they were looking for a particular retailer or item. In short, lifestyle centers reverse the model of the traditional mall where the anchor stores drew the traffic for the specialty stores. In the lifestyle centers, the specialty stores are the focus (Greg Lindsay, "Say Goodbye to the Mall," *Advertising Age*, October 2, 2006, p. 13).

How you develop your property depends on how you read trends such as these and your assumptions about how they might affect the performance of your project.

REFURBISHMENT OF TRUMP TAJ MAHAL
CASINO RESORT

"Now, as we near completion of the complete refurbishment of the Taj Mahal, we are able to offer our guests a uniquely elegant experience during their entire stay," summarized Mark Juliano,

(*continued*)

chief executive officer of Trump Entertainment Resorts. Projects completed include:

- The Penthouse Suites, an environment "defined by luxury."
- Il Mulino New York and Trattoria Il Mulino, two restaurants operated by Il Mulino, the number-one Italian restaurant in New York City for more than two decades, as rated by Zagat.
- Spice Road, a collection of shopping and dining experiences.
- High Limit Gaming Salon, two dozen tables for baccarat, blackjack, craps, and other high-limit games.
- Renovated casino floor with additional slot machines and gaming tables.

Managing your real estate brand requires continual management of your property values.

High Limit Gaming Salon, Trump Taj Mahal, Atlantic City.
Photo credit: Dominic Episcopo. Photo courtesy of the Trump Taj Mahal.

Source: "Famed Il Mulino New York Restaurant to Open at Trump Taj Mahal," Trump Taj Mahal press release, January 30, 2008.

Communicate Your Brand Position to Your Target Tenants   The communications tools available are similar to those discussed in Chapter 19:

- Identifiers—name, tag line, logo
- Signs and billboards
- Business cards and stationery
- Brochures
- Events
- Public relations
- Web site
- Direct mail
- Telemarketing
- In-person calls on customers or potential customers
- Print media
- Broadcast media
- Sales office and model units

These communications methods were discussed at length in prior chapters so we will not go over them again here.

NAMING THE REAL ESTATE BRAND

A name gives a property focus—so people can refer to it specifically rather than "the place I happen to live" or "where my store is."

You will find it worthwhile to spend time considering possible names. As always, you should keep the members of your target market in mind. The name should be descriptive, convey an image consistent with your brand position, and be distinctive from other names for similar properties in the area.

Neighborhood residents may be consulted as when Baywood Homes selected the name, "Bohemian Embassy," for their condominium project in a newly chic area. Baywood's sales and marketing manager declared, "We obviously wanted people to welcome it as part of their community. . . . We hired a PR firm to survey the local residents, businesses, and art galleries" (Derek Raymaker, "Playing Condo Name Game Can Be Tricky," *Globe and Mail*, November 17, 2006, p. G8).

CONCLUSION

The use of branding for properties has not been as widespread as for other types of products or services. One of the most notable exceptions is the Trump brand. The two principles of powerful branding—strong product and consistent message—have been employed relentlessly to build the Trump brand.

Branding your real estate properties improves your financial performance, attracts investors, and provides you with a solid growth platform for future projects.

(For more on managing real estate, see *Trump University Real Estate 101*, Hoboken, NJ: Wiley, 2006.)

V

Making Your Brand Work for You

21

How Brands Increase the
Value of a Business

B rands represent enormous amounts of money such as revenue, profits, and cash flow to organizations—if the brands are well-managed. Understanding how brands increase the value of business helps you decide how much time and money to spend on your brand efforts.

The relationship between brands and financial results is not magic. There is a simple chain linking brands and financial performance. That relationship is explained in this chapter.

What Is Brand Equity?

By "brand equity" we mean the value of a brand. How much it would be worth if you were to buy it.

Notice that for a brand to have value, there needs to be a potential buyer just as if a house has value, it is because someone is interested in buying it. We can estimate brand value but the actual value of a brand may differ by potential purchaser. An automobile manufacturer would probably be willing to pay more for Saab automobiles than would a manufacturer of pharmaceutical products—because the automobile manufacturer could do more with the Saab brand.

My definition of brand equity is based on thinking of a brand as an *asset*—just as you would value an invention or a factory. In finance, assets are evaluated in terms of the cash flows they can produce. That is how I define the value of a brand and what it contributes to a business—the cash flows it generates. My definition of brand equity:

> The net present value of the cash flows from a product or service with an established brand position less the cash flows from a comparable product or service without an established brand position.

This definition is completely consistent with how finance managers view the world. This definition is practical because it allows us to determine the value of a brand.

TRUMP INTERNATIONAL HOTEL & TOWER LAS VEGAS

The 64-story Trump International Hotel & Tower Las Vegas stands at the intersection of The Strip and Fashion Show Boulevard and will have 1,282 condominiums, a spa, a five-star restaurant, and luxurious amenities. Unveiled on *The Apprentice,* within a month, $10,000 deposits had been placed on 80 percent of the units. "Everybody wants to be in our building," Donald Trump explained to *BusinessWeek*.

In less than three years, construction was completed and it was completely sold out with sales of more than $1.1 billion.

Source: Christopher Palmeri, "Hike Your Odds on a Vegas Condo," *BusinessWeek,* February 14, 2005, p. 94.

Trump International Hotel & Tower
Las Vegas
Photo credit: Bergman Walls & Associates, 2005. Photo
courtesy of the Trump Organization.

Life Cycles

You can actually see brand equity by looking at the competitive life
cycle (which we discussed at length in Chapter 14). The product life cycle
(Exhibit 14.2) is a very familiar concept in marketing and branding.
It suggests how unit sales of a product or service change over time.

Margin, Costs, and Perceived Value

As you will remember from Chapter 14, margin per unit, defined as
price less unit cost, is typically negative in the Introduction stage, positive during the Rapid Growth stage, falls during Competitive Turbulence
due to price wars, remains steady for a while during Maturity, and then

falls again during the Decline stage. The cost per unit curve is usually high at the outset due to start-up costs and then falls as managers succeed in managing their operations.

Recall from Chapter 4 that perceived value per unit is the maximum the customer is willing to pay for your product or service. (That is why price premiums are inadequate as measures of brand equity even for a single customer as price premiums reflect both perceived value and pricing policy.) Perceived value can be measured in monetary terms—either subjectively or with quantitative techniques (called *constrained choice models*). Companies such as DuPont, Ford, and Marriott often estimate the perceived value of their products and services and use that information for their marketing and branding strategies.

Perceived value per unit begins relatively low, then increases during the Rapid Growth stage. Perceived value per unit declines during Competitive Turbulence as imitators enter then plateaus or declines slowly during the Maturity stage. Perceived value falls again throughout the Decline stage as products or services based on new and improved technologies enter the market.

Cash Flows Due to the Brand

The distance between the perceived value per unit curve and the cost per unit curve is *associated* with the margin curve. It is not the same as margin unless you are pricing to the maximum, but it is correlated with margin.

Similarly, the distance between the perceived value per unit curve and the cost per unit curve is *associated* with cash flow. Perceived value is associated with cash in and unit cost with cash out. This distance is not equivalent to cash flow but determines cash flow.

To see brand equity, consider the perceived value curve as corresponding to a product or service that is an established brand. Compare that perceived value curve to the perceived value curve for a product or service without an established brand (see Exhibit 21.1). The distance between these curves is associated with the difference in their

Exhibit 21.1   Brand Equity

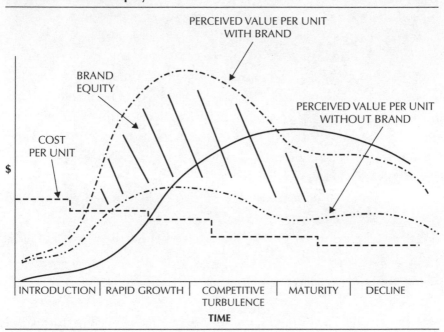

Source: "Arrow Guide—Value Brand Equity," The Arrow Group, Ltd.®, New York, 2008. Used with permission.

cash flows, adjusted also by any cost differences between the branded and unbranded product or service.

In short, the higher the perceived value per unit of the branded product or service and the lower the cost per unit, the higher the cash flow to your organization. You can increase cash flow either by increasing perceived value or decreasing costs or both.

Higher perceived value and lower costs per unit increase cash flow.

Brands are an important component of cash flow. As Chivas Regal pointed out in one of their global advertising campaigns, "Either you have it [a strong brand] or you don't."

You either have it
or you don't

Those who appreciate quality enjoy it responsibly

Chivas Regal two-page advertisement.

The stronger your brand, the stronger your financial performance.

TRUMP INTERNATIONAL HOTEL & TOWER CHICAGO

High perceived value allows you to charge high prices because you are providing high value to your customers—a known gold standard brand turns an intangible into a tangible. The sales of units in the Chicago Trump International Hotel & Tower were a major cause of a 30 percent increase in the average price of new townhome and condominium units in the Chicago area during the last quarter of 2003.

The units in the planned Trump International Hotel & Tower accounted for almost 30 percent of the sales of luxury condominiums, according to Tracy Cross, president of Tracy Cross & Associates, Inc., which tracks the prices of housing in the Chicago area. Prices of units in the Trump building started at about a half million dollars—top units were selling for over $11 million.

**Trump International Hotel & Tower
Chicago**
Photo credit: Skidmore Owings & Merrill,
2005. Photo courtesy of the Trump Organization.

The average price for all townhome/condo units in the Chicago area during the quarter was $340,000.

The Trump Organization estimates the Trump name on a building results in a price lift of 50 to 60 percent.

As one reporter observed, "Call it the Donald effect."

Source: Alby Gallun, "City's Average Home Price Gets a Bump from Trump," *Crain's Chicago Business,* February 2, 2004.

Sources of Brand Value

How do brands increase the value of a business?

Foremost is their impact on customer behavior as shown in the competitive life cycle. Strong brands lead customers to try your product or service, repurchase, and be willing to pay a higher price for it due to its higher perceived value. Customers also recommend brands they like to others and, in times of crises, are often loyal to their brands.

Because of their clout with customers and consumers, strong brands provide your business with the power to fight competitors and to make favorable deals with resellers.

Strong brands also lead to lower costs. Once a brand is well-known and well-accepted, it is no longer in a building mode but in a maintenance mode. Communications expenditures will then be more efficient.

Often ignored by those valuing brands is the impact of a strong brand on your employees. I was working with a software company in Silicon Valley where people often switch organizations. One of the managers in my group said that their strong brand was invaluable both in recruiting and retaining the most able employees. Strong brands also increase the morale of employees because they are proud and possessive of their organization's reputation.

Strong brands increase employee morale—human resources managers should be strong supporters of branding efforts.

The most difficult aspect of valuing a brand concerns its potential to grow—to be extended to other products and services (Chapter 12). Both of us can be looking at the same brand but you may consider it to be more valuable than I because you see more possible growth options that can be based on the brand. That is a main reason why you cannot really talk about the value of a brand unless you have a buyer in mind. Two companies may value a brand quite differently. Each may see different possibilities in the brand and each may have different skills for exploiting the brand as an asset.

Conclusion

There are strong arguments as to why brands are valuable and, consequently, why you must devote energy to managing your brand. In studies by the Conference Board ("Managing the Corporate Brand," New York, 1998) and the American Productivity and Quality Center ("Brand Building and Communication," Houston, 1999), one of the characteristics found to distinguish companies successfully managing their brands from those that were not was a concern to understand exactly how their brands led to improved financial results. That understanding allowed them to make more successful branding decisions and to persuade others of the need to devote resources to their branding efforts. You *can* increase the value of your business through your brand.

22

CONSTRUCTING THE
SCORECARD FOR
YOUR BRAND

You need to monitor your brand over time so you know when to change your efforts or modify your strategy. The measures you use to monitor your brand are known as the *brand scorecard*.

Numerous measures have been suggested to monitor the health of a brand. Are all of these measures really necessary? Is there a smaller group of measures that can form an effective brand scorecard? What should you look at to keep track of how your brand is doing?

BUILDING THE BRAND SCORECARD

For a year, I worked with members of the Conference Board's Council on Corporate Brand Management to build a brand scorecard that would consist of a smaller set of measures. Throughout the process, many brand managers provided feedback as to what measures should be selected.

We started by looking at all the many measures that have been proposed and creating an inventory of brand measures. Next, we set up criteria to determine whether a measure should be included in the scorecard. Brand managers were asked to evaluate all the measures based on their experience as to what worked and what did not and what measures were informative and what measures were not. The scorecard was constructed with the measures receiving the highest evaluations.

Brand managers were asked what measures worked for them.

The scorecard that resulted provides a comprehensive view of the health of a brand—and requires only eight measures.

BRAND MEASURE INVENTORY

The initial inventory of brand measures was developed by looking at a great variety of sources. Measures came from brand managers, advertising agencies, consulting firms, industry organizations, professors, authors, and journalists.

In total, well over 100 measures were found that had been proposed by someone somewhere sometime. However, some measures were very similar to others such as repeat purchase, retention, and loyalty. After consolidating the measures, there were 32 measures for consideration.

Criteria for Inclusion in Scorecard

An effective scorecard must consist of measures that will be useful. Several criteria were applied to evaluate the list of 32 measures, including:

- *Understandable:* Some consultancies use measures that are difficult if not impossible to decipher. Useful measures should be clear and easy to explain.

- *Measurable:* Any measure must be operational. There must be practical ways to estimate the measure over time.
- *Actionable:* A measure must provide information for decisions.
- *Brand-related:* The measure must describe some aspect or consequence of a brand.
- *Holistic:* All the aspects or consequences of a brand should be covered by the scorecard measures.
- *Cover all constituencies:* Provide evaluation for brand performance with all audiences.
- *Cover all sources of brand value:* Allow monitoring of all ways brands create value.
- *Effective:* Proven to work in practice.
- *Overall framework:* The set of scorecard measures should cover all aspects of the branding process so that the scorecard can provide guidance for developing brand strategy and implementing brand strategy.

EVALUATION OF MEASURES

Many brand managers—members of the Council on Corporate Brand Management—were asked what they considered to be the important measures to use in the scorecard and those measures they considered crucial to use in the scorecard.

The survey did not employ random sampling so cannot be considered representative of the opinions of all brand managers. However, the twenty or so participants control many of the most significant and valuable brands in the world and their opinions should be of considerable interest.

The overall winner was perceived value (see Exhibit 22.1). That finding is quite consistent with many studies by organizations such as Corebrand, Young & Rubicam, and the Strategic Planning Institute that have found perceived value to be a *leading* indicator of profits, cash flow, and shareholder value. The finding is also very consistent with my own empirical work on valuing brands.

Exhibit 22.1   Brand Scorecard Measures

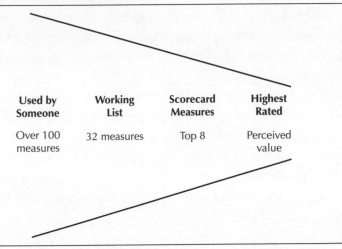

Used by Someone	Working List	Scorecard Measures	Highest Rated
Over 100 measures	32 measures	Top 8	Perceived value

Source: Donald E. Sexton, "Building the Brand Scorecard," *Advertiser,* February 2005, pp. 54–58.

> **If you have to choose just one measure to monitor
> your brand, chose perceived value.**

There were seven other winning measures for inclusion in a brand scorecard:

1. Name recall
2. Differentiation
3. Relevance
4. Trust
5. Brand trial
6. Customer satisfaction
7. Recommend

Four measures focus on the components of a brand. Name recall measures the strength of the identifier. Differentiation measures performance on the attributes of the product or service. Relevance measures the importance of the attributes. Trust measures the strength of the associations.

The other three measures focus on different stages in the purchase process. Brand trial refers to initial purchase. Customer satisfaction measures performance of the product or service in use. Recommend measures the postpurchase willingness of the customer to suggest the product or service to someone else.

Missing from this list of eight measures are popular measures such as "ad recall," "price premium," and "purchase intent" as well as most of the 100-plus measures with which we started.

Certainly other similar measures might replace some of the measures we included in the brand scorecard. However, a process that started with a long list of possible measures ended with a remarkably short list.

CONCLUSION

You don't need a hundred measures to monitor your brand. In fact, you can obtain an excellent idea of the strength of your brand with just one measure—perceived value. However, you may want to track the components of perceived value and different stages in the purchase cycle. We found eight measures that seemed to be both comprehensive and practical.

23

YOUR EMPLOYEES AND
YOUR BRAND

If employees understand the brand, they can support the brand (see Exhibit 23.1). Employees' actions, in turn, can have a considerable effect on how the organization is viewed by current and prospective customers, by current and prospective employees, and by current and prospective investors.

Brands can be a key instrument in setting the tone for company culture that affects employee actions—both during normal times and during times of change. In normal times, the brand provides employees with direction for performing well. In times of change, brands may be even more critical as they can give stability to an organization by providing employees with guidelines for their actions.

Exhibit 23.1   Employees and the Brand

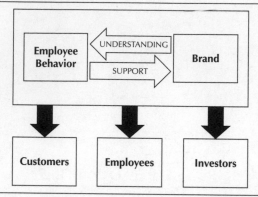

Source: "Arrow Guide—Employees and the Brand," The Arrow Group, Ltd.®, New York, 2008. Used with permission.

TRUMP HOTEL COLLECTION NEW EMPLOYEE ORIENTATION

Managers of the Trump Hotel Collection provide new employees with an understanding of the philosophy of the hotels and the meaning and significance of the brand. During their orientation meetings, along with specifics such as policies and procedures, new employees learn:

- History of Trump Family
- Overview of Trump Hotel Collection
- What Makes a Great Brand
- Culture including Values and Mission
- Guest Service Philosophy
- Organization's Expectations and Role of Employee
- Measurements Used to Determine Performance

The initial orientation takes two days with follow-up sessions 30 days and 90 days afterward.

Trump International Hotel & Tower New York City.
Photo credit: Jon Ortner, 2002. Photo courtesy of the Trump
Organization.

These meetings are designed to ensure that all employees understand what the Trump Hotel Collection brand stands for and their role in building the brand. Associates do not start work until they have attended the New Employee Orientation.

Source: Trump Hotel Collection internal document, April 23, 2007.

YOUR EMPLOYEES AND YOUR BRAND

Especially in service companies, the employees are the face of the brand to the customers. Companies with powerful brands such as Starbucks, Southwest Airlines, UPS, Ritz Carlton, FPL, and jetBlue credit much of their success to their employees' understanding of and belief in their brands and their willingness to build and reinforce their brands in all their contacts with customers.

However, even in companies that produce products, such as automobiles or computers, employee support of the company brand may have significant impact on reliability and other attributes of the products produced. Toyota and Apple employees are famously supportive of their company's brands.

Your employees are the face of your brand.

Employees who support a company's brands not only help that company attract and retain their target customers, by setting examples they also help the company attract and retain target employees—those employees the organization values most. In Silicon Valley, there is considerable competition for skilled employees. Companies with strong brands such as Oracle, Yahoo!, Cisco, and Google have an advantage when they are recruiting or when they are trying to keep valued employees.

Finally, employee understanding and support of the brand can help an organization appeal to investors. Companies that have had crises resulting in considerable management change, such as Tyco, have employed their brand as part of their efforts to renew their organizations and increase their attractiveness to the financial community.

A study by The Conference Board ("Managing the Corporate Brand," New York, 1998) suggested that communication of brand identity standards, employee ability to describe the brand, and employee performance standards linked to the brand were among the practices that most distinguished those companies which The Conference Board considered to be those following "best practices" in branding. A similar study by the American Productivity and Quality Center ("Brand Building and Communication," Houston, 1999) found that practices such as having a branding policy manual, employee brand understanding, and brand-related compensation were among the most important differentiating practices of what they believed were branding "best practice" companies.

Studies show that in best-practice branding organizations, employees understand their brand.

While brands can provide employees with direction, especially in times of change, familiarizing the employees with the brand and, more importantly, persuading them to live the brand may require substantial effort. Effective ways to communicate the brand to employees and encourage them to support the brand include:

- The brand book
- Brand presentations
- Branding key performance indicators (KPIs)

The Brand Book

Most organizations have a style guide that sets forth the color and fonts to be used in all mentions of the brand. It may also include guidelines for developing different kinds of advertising. Often the keeper of the style guide—rather unfairly—may be referred to as the "logo cop."

A style guide is *not* what is meant by a brand book—although it may be part of a brand book.

Organizations such as GE, Wachovia, Harley-Davidson, Caterpillar, and the Hallmark Channel define the contents of their brand books to be much broader in scope than the conventional style guide. They make sure that they first explain to the employees *why* branding is important before providing them with detailed instructions as to what the logo should look like and where it should be placed on a page.

Generally brand books consist of three major parts (Exhibit 23.2):

1. Reasons for branding
2. Description of the brand
3. How to maintain the brand

Exhibit 23.2 The Brand Book

Part I: Reasons for Branding

Brand values
    World's most valuable brands
    Value of our brand

The Value of Brands
    Value to customers
    Value to organizations

How Valuable Brands Are Built and Maintained
    Consistency over time and over markets
    Brand understanding and discipline

Role of Employees in Building and Maintaining the Brand

Part II: Description of Our Brand

What Is a Brand?
    Identifiers
    Attributes
    Associations

What Does Our Brand Stand For?
    Our brand's logo and other identifiers
    Key benefits of our brand
    Key associations—the brand promise

Who Are Our Target Customers?
    Demographics or other descriptors
    Needs of the target customers

Our Brand Promise
    Significance to our target customers
    How we will keep the promise

Part III: How We Maintain Our Brand

Speaking with One Brand Voice
    Tone and manner
    Logo style guide

Exhibit 23.2   The Brand Book (Continued)

Graphic element style guide
Font style guide
Advertising style guide
[Other style guides]

How to Be a Brand Champion

Appendices:

Frequently Asked Questions

Checklist for Brand Communications (dos and don'ts)

Source: "Arrow Guide—Employees and the Brand," The Arrow Group, Ltd.®, New York, 2008. Used with permission.

Part I, the reasons for branding, provides employees with the rationale for the company's branding efforts. Typically it would include some of the publicly available figures concerning the monetary values of the most valuable brands in the world and, if available, the estimated value of the company's brand.

Next might be an explanation as to why brands are valuable. They are valuable to customers because they signal attributes that the customers wish to purchase. They are valuable to organizations because they lead to revenue, profits, and cash flow.

Finally, part I might include a discussion of the importance of consistency and discipline in building a brand and the role of employees in keeping the company's brand promise.

The purpose of the Part II, description of the company's brand, is to convey to the employees the crucial attributes of the brand.

Part II might begin with a definition of what a brand is. For example, a brand can be considered to consist of identifiers (name, logo), attributes (benefits), and associations (connections between the identifiers and attributes). Then each of those brand components can be specified for the organization's brand.

For example, an automobile repair shop might use a drawing of an automobile as their logo. Their key attributes might be availability (24-hour service) and expertise ("our mechanics know every make of car as if it were their own"). The brand promise might describe how the company will make clear to customers that they can be sure they will obtain the benefits linked to the brand.

Part II might also contain a reminder of who the target customers are and what their needs are. That would lead to a discussion that develops the idea of the brand promise, why it is important to the target customers, and how the promise will be kept. Perhaps customer testimonials might be included.

Part III describes how the brand will be maintained and might begin with qualitative comments concerning the tone and manner of any brand communication (e.g., exciting, neighborly, experienced). Most of Part III would be the style guide. In fact, there may be many style guides—for the logo, for graphics, for fonts. However, now the employee knows the reason for the style guide—to build a brand with consistency—and hopefully will now be more inclined to take actions to support the brand.

Part III might also include a section on how to be a brand champion. This might include suggestions as to how to advocate the brand internally and how to embody the brand externally—to customers in particular.

Some organizations include appendices in their brand books that contain a list of frequently asked questions or perhaps a checklist for evaluating any brand communication (specifications of font, color, etc.).

BRAND PRESENTATIONS

You cannot expect employees to become disciples of the brand just by reading through the brand book—however well-written and well-designed it might be. Persuading employees to live the brand requires a consistent internal sell and that includes presentations.

The presentations need not be more than an hour, but they should be scheduled so that everyone has an opportunity to attend one of them. A senior executive should be present throughout each session. They should introduce the session but then they should remain throughout the session to indicate clearly that they feel the branding efforts are important.

The agenda for the session might follow somewhat the outline for the brand book (Exhibit 23.3). However, it can be quite effective to employ various media in the presentation such as videos of the company's

Exhibit 23.3   Brand Presentation

– Introduction

– Reasons for Branding
   Values of brands
   Why brands are valuable
   How to build and maintain brands

– Description of Our Brand
   Definition of a brand
   What our brand stands for
   Importance of our brand promise to our target customer

– How We Maintain Our Brand
   Need for consistency
   Need for style guides
   How to be a brand champion

Source: "Arrow Guide—Employees and the Brand," The Arrow Group, Ltd.®, New York, 2008. Used with permission.

advertisements or activities. Videos of customers (and perhaps employees) talking about the company and the brand can have considerable impact. If customer videos are used, it is important that there be a mix of positive comments and other comments spotlighting where the organization might improve its efforts in keeping the brand promise.

When I was helping a large electrical utility develop their brand, we conducted several sessions for all their "wires and poles" people— the operations people who often embodied the brand to the customers— to explain to them the importance of their branding efforts.

Key Performance Indicators

Communicating the brand position will likely not be sufficient to convince every employee to live the brand. Branding efforts need to be tied to key performance indicators and then to rewards such as compensation, promotions, or recognition.

There are a multitude of brand measures available. One set of possible measures for a brand scorecard was developed by members of the

Council on Corporate Brand Management of The Conference Board during a year-long process that I facilitated (see Chapter 22).

Among the more than 100 measures considered for the scorecard, perceived value was easily the measure most favored by the group of corporate brand managers. The next four measures—name recall, differentiation, relevance, and trust—measure the different components of a brand and the other three measures—brand trial, customer satisfaction, and recommend—track different stages of the purchase and use cycle.

These are certainly not the only measures that might be used, but they do represent a parsimonious and coherent set of measures of brand performance. If you want employees to support the brand, brand performance must be measured. The well-known rule—what is measured is managed, what is not measured is not managed—applies here.

The brand measures can then be linked to various rewards. While compensation and promotions are certainly important rewards, recognition can also be very effective. A letter from a senior executive or a mention of an employee's name at an important meeting can do much to encourage brand support.

CONCLUSION

An organization's brands are typically its most valuable single asset. The values of those brands often depend on how employees live the brand and how they keep the brand promise, especially with customers. In addition, brands are an important aspect of organization culture and can be used to help organizations through periods of change.

For employees to support the brand, they must fully understand the brand and they must be rewarded for their actions in support of the brand. That requires effective internal brand communications and an objectively based reward system to encourage the desired brand efforts.

Hopefully you have found ideas in this book that you can put to immediate use to strengthen your brands and increase your revenues, profits, and cash flows. May all your brands be strong!

DON SEXTON

INDEX

INDEX

PERSONAL GOALS:

- ☑ Get promoted.
- ☑ Fire my boss.
- ☑ Start my own business.
- ☑ Buy a home.
- ☑ Flip a home.
- ☑ Enjoy financial independence.
- ☑ Live larger.
- ☑ Laugh more.
- ☑ Achieve my dreams.

START RIGHT HERE:
www.TrumpUniversity.com

Donald Trump knows about success. He lives it. He epitomizes it. And now he's ready to *teach* it — with world-class instructors, convenient online learning programs, and a wealth of streetwise wealth-building wisdom that can give you a lifelong professional and personal advantage.

Visit our website today — **www.TrumpUniversity.com** to learn more, do more, and BE more. The information is absolutely free — but the opportunity could be priceless.